We recognise and appreciate the lived experience of collaborators across our co-design teams, partners and clients. Their expertise, creativity and insights inform and inspire our ongoing practice.

BIS Publishers
Borneostraat 80-A
1094 CP Amsterdam
The Netherlands

T +31 (0)20 515 02 30 | bis@bispublishers.com | www.bispublishers.com
ISBN 978-90-636-9692-4

Graphic design by Jessica Cheers and Jeremy Kerr

Copyedited by Abbe Winter and Rebecca Cheers

Photography on inner cover and pages 1, 3, 5, 13, 18, 19, 43, 247, 252, 259, 282, 283, 286, 291, 297, 303, 309 and 311 by Anthony Hearsey

Figurine images by Jessica Cheers and Anthony Hearsey

Additional images by Jessica Cheers

This project was made possible by seed funding provided for the CCNR Co-Design Framework and Toolkit by the Children's Hospital Foundation, with generous support from Woolworths staff and customers. The CCNR was established in 2018 by founding partners Woolworths and Children's Hospital Foundation thanks to the generosity of Woolworth's' customers and team members.

the
art of
co-design

BISPUBLISHERS

Jeremy Kerr
Jessica Cheers
Danielle Gallegos
Alethea Blackler
Nick Kelly

0   hello!

1   why co-design?

2   being a co-designer

6   doing co-design

7   analysing + sensemaking

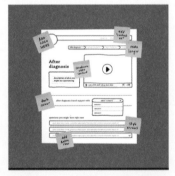

8   prototyping + testing

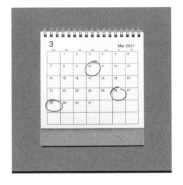

3 designing for co-design

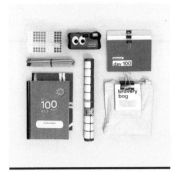

4 A-Z of methods

5 getting ready to co-design

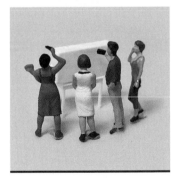

9 co-developing + co-implementing

10 evaluating + exploring possibilities

11 bringing it all together

what's inside

why we co-design

When I started working as a designer, to be successful seemed to require simply having a strong empathy and connection with consumers. Back then, the process of "problem-framing" and designing "solutions" was very much driven by the idea of stepping into someone else's shoes. However, when faced with particularly challenging design problems, I often wondered: "what if I could just ask the people I'm designing for what they *really* need and want?" At the time, it didn't feel like an appropriate thing to do; how could I be a credible designer if I was relying on others to come up with the solution for me? On the other hand, maybe this approach could lead to something much better than what I'd come up with singlehandedly.

While designers typically wear a "design guru" hat, I felt very conflicted in such a role. We seldom have all the answers and do a lot of guessing. As I ventured into new sectors, particularly into social change, I kept wondering if there was another way to design – something that could allow us to understand, care and innovate even more. I was heartened when I found it. Designing with people at the centre of a design, not simply designing for them: *co-design*. It seemed like a lot of people were contemplating this approach at the same time. After exploring it, I have never looked back. It just feels the right way to design – and I'm consistently struck by how ingenious the outcomes continue to be. Co-design has allowed me to engage with people in profound ways and work on problems that seemed unsolvable. I've had the opportunity and privilege to collaborate with diverse groups of people – people processing trauma, people living with a disability, young children, and those experiencing homelessness – addressing their unique challenges to create change.

Working with these collaborators means engaging with *true* experts – those with lived experience. As a designer, I now find myself creating opportunities for others' voices to be heard. My role is to ignite their creativity, working together to solve the problems that affect them. I facilitate, interpret, suggest, provoke, and support collaboration, using my creativity at key points, but supporting others to take the lead. Co-design is a hard process to explain, which is why this book exists. It's our passionate attempt to demystify something people can be apprehensive or skeptical of, until they are part of the process in action. Co-design is a future-focused, rewarding, and unpredictable new field of design – I hope this book excites you about its possibilities!

My evolution from capital-D Designer to co-designer has been humbling, heartening, curious and surprising. I cut my chops as a graphic designer, imagining I'd be pushing pixels in a design studio from 9-5. It wasn't long before I started to feel disenchanted with the work I was doing – I was finding myself making arbitrary decisions in isolation, struggling to find meaning and connect with a "why". Around this time, I was approached by a research team who was developing a mental health toolkit with the largest youth phone counselling service in Australia and needed a design lead. Weeks later I was unexpectedly thrust into a confronting and captivating two-year crash course in co-design. Suddenly, I was facilitating my first collaborative workshops, working alongside 30 young people, counsellors and psychologists to bring their ideas to life.

My first experience with co-design sparked as many "aha!" moments as "huh?" moments. On the one hand, I was hooked. I found it impossible to return to my old way of doing things – I loved untangling complex problems, I loved working alongside the people who experienced those problems first-hand, and I loved creating tools and spaces that empowered people to reflect on their experiences and express their ideas. At the same time, I felt ill-equipped as a co-design facilitator. I quickly noticed that the more playful, creative and subversive the activities, the more participants felt comfortable experimenting with new ideas. However, I had no idea how to craft compelling co-design spaces, let alone which methods to use and why. I wanted to dig deeper into the kind of methods and tactile tools that could support meaningful (and fun!) creative collaboration, while also inspiring usable and sustainable solutions. Our "A-Z of methods" is my labour of love, something that would have saved me a few years of trial and error at the beginning of my co-design crusade.

I've since found a home in healthcare, with no shortage of wicked problems to explore. Whether I'm working with people in the last months of their lives or children with juvenile arthritis, my role is to create an engaging co-design experience, listening and adapting to their needs. What excites me most about co-design is the chance to take a humble step back and get the basics right: to be curious, ask thoughtful questions, and discover unexpected opportunities to improve some of the most emotionally affecting moments in a person's life. At its best, co-design isn't just about creating shiny solutions – it brings people with shared lived experience together, creates communities and turns challenging experiences into meaningful change. I hope that our enthusiasm for co-design is infectious, and that you put down this book feeling curious, crafty and full of new ideas.

who we are

The Art of Co-design emerged from a research project within the Centre for Childhood Nutrition Research in Queensland, Australia. The centre was founded on an ethos of community engagement, child and family-led innovation and creative problem-solving, making co-design a natural fit. We were tasked with working alongside the centre's nutrition researchers to develop a series of co-design resources, creating the tools they needed to apply co-design to their projects, authentically and ethically. In our quest to meet the needs of healthcare researchers, we realised that many other contexts were also craving practical co-design resources. Before we knew it, we had created a universal co-design handbook, rich with creative methods that could be adapted to any context.

Nick Kelly
studies the cognition of creativity and brings these ideas into the world of education

PROJECT TEAM

Alethea Blackler
is a leading expert in intuitive interaction, conducting research with a diverse range of people, from children to the elderly

PROJECT TEAM

Danielle Gallegos
brings innovation to the child and community health sectors through citizen-led design

PROJECT TEAM

This book builds on our team's collective knowledge of co-design practices and methods, developed through years of collaboration with diverse groups and communities. In creating this handbook we embarked on a systematic review of co-design literature and resources, reflected on our own research and community projects, and facilitated co-design workshops with researchers and health professionals to understand what tools they needed to bring their own co-design projects to life. We think of this book as a celebration of emerging design methods and the potential of collaborative design. It's the resource we wish we had when we were starting out: a no-nonsense, flexible and practical guide to making co-design work in the wild. Alongside this book, we have also created an online resource that is freely available, making co-design accessible to all: **www.co-designer.co**

Jessica Cheers

advocates for the use of playful, creative and provocative methods in untangling complex problems, and is currently on a crusade to humanise healthcare through co-design

AUTHOR + DESIGNER

Jeremy Kerr

champions the design of new methods and models to magnify the creative voices of marginalised and underrepresented communities

AUTHOR + DESIGNER

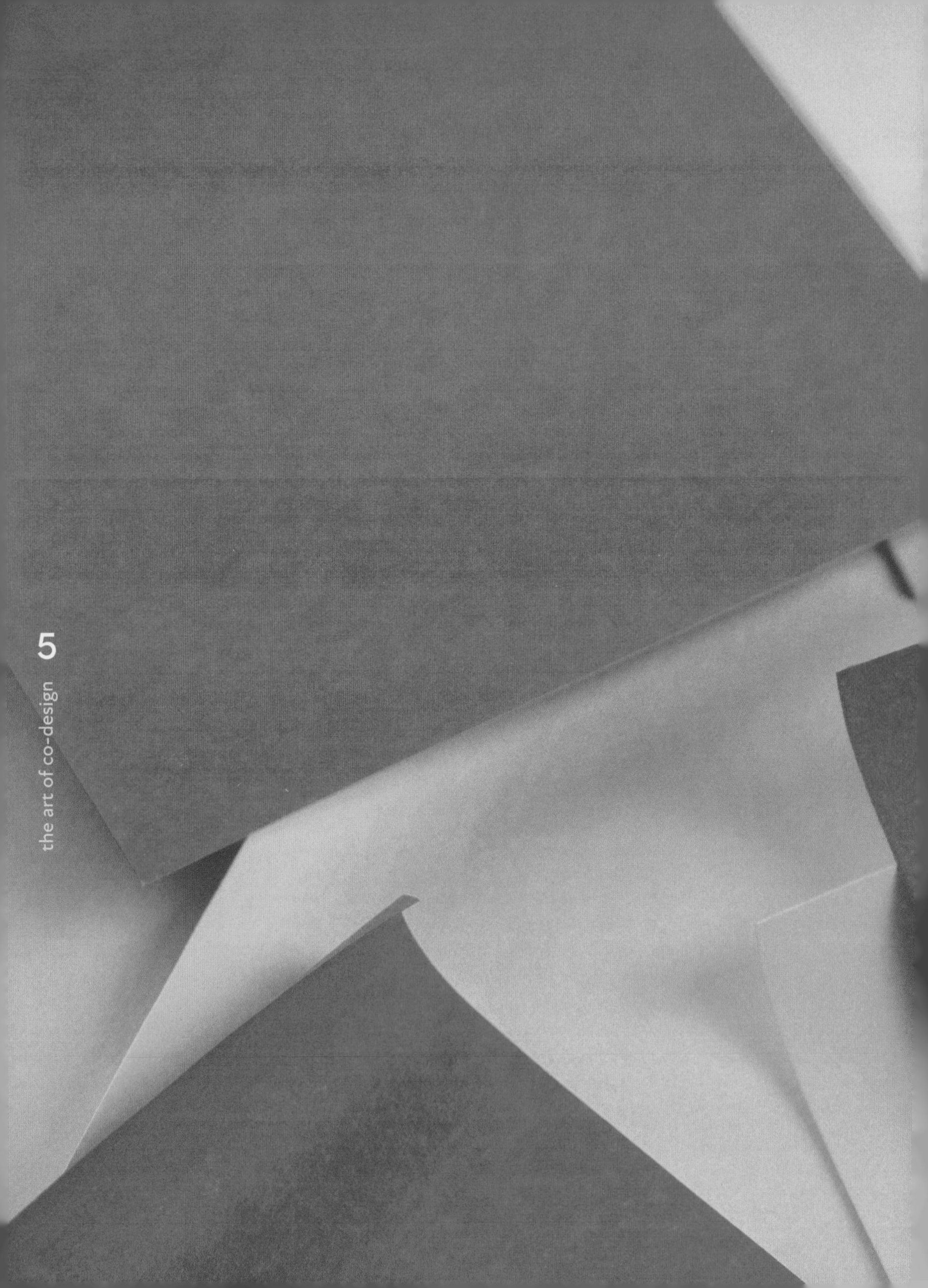

why co-design?

If you're here, you've likely heard the word *"co-design"* before. Co-design is growing in popularity, yet in many cases it's still poorly understood. The following section covers the co-design basics: *what* it is, *where* it came from and *why* it's worth doing.

what is co-design?

Co-design is designing with people, not for them

CO-DESIGN HAPPENS WITH PEOPLE WHO ARE DIRECTLY AFFECTED BY WHAT IS BEING DESIGNED

Co-design celebrates people as experts of their own lived experience

CO-DESIGN CREATES SPACE FOR PEOPLE TO RESPOND TO THE PROBLEMS AND OPPORTUNITIES THAT AFFECT THEM

Co-design is a design-led method of collaboration that uses creative and participatory methods

Co-design is inherently complex, messy and exploratory

CO-DESIGN IS A CRUCIAL APPROACH TO ADDRESSING COMPLEX ISSUES AND SOLVING 'WICKED' PROBLEMS

Co-design is being used to innovate systems, services, initiatives, buildings and products

co-design is happening more and more in government, health, education and business sectors

what does co-design look like?

Co-design starts with a core co-design team identifying a challenge or opportunity, then assembling relevant people (i.e. stakeholders) to collaborate. This generally occurs within *creative workshops* with representatives of a stakeholder group or mixed stakeholder groups. The workshops, led by a facilitator or facilitators, consist of linked activities, based on reflective and generative methods. These activities often involve sketching and making to bring about insights and ideas which the co-design team can review and respond to. Follow-up co-design sessions then allow a project to be further developed and refined, using diverse methods.

While *in-person workshops* are the most popular in the field, they are increasingly being held *online* or in a *blended* format (with a combination of in-person and online participants). As well as these *synchronous* workshops, co-design projects often make use of *asynchronous* co-design activities that stakeholders can complete in their own time, offering additional opportunities for creative collaboration.

While it is common for a co-design team to engage stakeholders extensively in the ideation and prototyping process, it is less so that they are actively involved in developing and implementing solutions. This more holistic approach to co-design is being increasingly pursued, however, as it is seen as a more ethical way to collaborate. There is growing evidence demonstrating this leads to more successful outcomes.

what is
co-design
similar to?

we will keep you informed, take on your feedback and let you know how it was incorporated in what we decided to do

consultation

extractive

design thinking

is a series of strategies and practical processes allowing designers to prioritise a consumer – or user – when developing products and services, and many of these methods are now used within co-design

focus groups

are a way for organisations to engage stakeholders around specific topics, limited to direct answers and conversation with little opportunity to creatively develop outcomes

PAR

or "participatory action researc infers a continuous partnership with stakeholders – it is sometimes seen as a larger leve of engagement than co-design which is often project-based

There are a number of other approaches that are based on stakeholder engagement and employ similar methods. While definitions for each are not entirely agreed upon, below are some of the most commonly used terms. In comparing co-design to other types of engagement, it's important to recognise that co-design sits on a spectrum of approaches for working with stakeholders. While not as collaborative as co-design, these are still valid and valuable ways for partnering with stakeholders.

let's work together to understand and solve this problem from start to finish

co-design

→

empowering

open design

is a movement that is centred on collaboration occurring through the use of publicly-shared design information, such as open-source software

co-creation

encompasses any act of collective creativity, and typically involves "one-off" events rather than ongoing collaborative partnerships

co-production

infers an ongoing and continuous partnership with stakeholders; it is sometimes seen as a larger level of engagement than co-design, which tends to be project-based

where did co-design come from?

While co-design is synonymous with innovation today, its foundations emerged decades ago. Co-design has been championed by people across the world in a range of contexts. This is a brief origin story, describing three snapshots in time.

60s - 70s

80s - 90s

today

The origins of co-design have been linked to widespread moves, throughout the 1960s and 70s, to integrate community views and opinions into decision-making processes. Specific participatory design methods emerged in Scandinavia in the 1970s with the development of cooperative design, which came with unique techniques and approaches to engage stakeholders in design processes. Cooperative design was based on collective problem-solving, allowing workers to have input into the technology systems that they used every day.

Following early success, the ideology and approach of designing with, not for, has continued into sectors such as education, health and software design through the 1980s and beyond. Methods like future workshops and low fidelity prototyping emerged during this era, promoting speculative and hands-on approaches to collaboration.

The benefits of this collaborative approach have been proven, and it has been applied to an array of organisations, industries and contexts. Today the process has evolved to be called "co-design", and it continues to grow in scope and possibilities. Co-design projects now routinely engage multiple stakeholder groups in collaboration, including consumers, community members, staff, industry experts, potential users and policy-makers.

why do we co-design?

IT PRODUCES SOLUTIONS THAT ARE MORE LIKELY TO MEET USER'S NEEDS

it creates more sustainable solutions

it supports community buy-in and builds relationships

it allows for unforseen and unexpected needs and priorities to be met

IT CREATES AN ENVIRONMENT FOR ONGOING COLLABORATION

IT'S INCLUSIVE RATHER THAN TOP-DOWN

it supports organisations to build empathy

it promotes creativity and novel solutions

it leverages collective intelligence

13

being a co-designer

Co-design is not just a collection of tools and methods, but an approach to collaboration that relies on shared values and mindsets. The following section steps into the mind of a co-designer, highlighting *12 values* and *5 designer* mindsets that underpin any successful co-design team.

values

Great co-design teams are built on shared values. We've found the following to be the most essential to creative collaboration.

respect

Co-design is built on a foundation of mutual respect: observing people's feelings and rights, and accepting them for who they are regardless of differences. Sometimes respect may be represented in co-design through payment for a participant's time. Respect also means acknowledging and recognising people's contributions.

valuing lived experience

A person's lived experience is just as important as an expert's knowledge and experience. Everyone is an expert on their own experience, and working with people with lived experience can be just as valuable as working with experts in a field.

equality

Equality means recognising the value of all knowledges and working together as equals for the common good. This may mean consciously breaking down traditional power relationships and hierarchies between different stakeholder groups. For example, in health, it may entail ensuring both clinical staff and those with lived experience of a health condition see each other as equal experts, with knowledge and skills that are complementary.

inclusiveness

The more diverse voices engaged in co-design, the richer and more productive the process will be. This means continually asking "who's missing?", including marginalised groups, and seeking diversity in relation to age, gender, socio-economic situation, cultural background and abilities. A co-design team should establish an environment where all feel truly welcome.

trusting relationships

Through embodying respect and promoting equality, co-design builds relationships based on trust, establishing a strong foundation for ongoing partnerships. Relationships are integral to a successful creative problem-solving process, increasing the openness of people and encouraging authenticity, honesty and vulnerability.

shared decision-making

Without sharing decisions and power within a project, there is no co-design. Letting go of control as a co-design team and allowing participants to be equal partners in the decision-making process is crucial to enacting the principle: "nothing about us, without u

strength-based

Strength-based approaches focus on an individual's strengths, and not on their deficits or weaknesses. This means framing things from a positive perspective, viewing people as resilient, resourceful, and strong. Taking this approach throughout co-design supports the wellbeing of participants and creates an environment free of critique or judgement.

capacity building

A natural result of the co-design process is that participants are likely to feel an increased sense of creative confidence, while also learning about the topic being explored and the process of co-design itself. In this way, co-design can be mutually beneficial, assisting a co-design team in finding a solution while also equipping participants with new skills and knowledge and expanding their sense of self. Participants may go on to co-author research outcomes, become co-facilitators on subsequent projects, or even lead their own co-design teams.

everyone can be creative

Everyone can be a designer, and everyone can contribute meaningfully to solving problems that relate to themselves in innovative ways, given the right resources, tools and supports. This is the role of the co-designer: to create environments in which a participant's natural creativity can flourish.

playfulness

Cultivating a playful collaborative environment creates space for innovative and unexpected ideas to emerge. The design process can be intrinsically fun, exciting and exuberant, and even serious issues can be explored in playful ways. Play can emerge through the tone of the facilitator (upbeat and enthusiastic), the way the environment is created (in a relaxing, colourful and tactile space, considering elements like background music) and in the way activities are designed.

authentic collaboration

Co-design means making together and working towards a collective solution. Co-design methods should not be about relaying information but facilitating discovery and supporting active participation in the design process. An ethos of "designing together" should be core to project design, avoiding tokenism and superficial participation. Participants should be engaged authentically throughout all stages of a project, from ideation to implementation.

trauma-informed

Trauma-informed approaches prioritise wellbeing by acknowledging that many participants' lived experienced may involve traumatic events. People are then engaged in ways that consciously avoid upsetting or further traumatising them. There is an ethos of "do no harm" and this means ensuring people feel safe, promoting trust, providing transparency, offering support if needed and giving participants autonomy over their involvement at all times.

mindsets

This "designerly" mindset can come naturally to some, while for others it can be at odds with how you work and live. You don't need to be a designer to be a co-designer. However, making a conscious effort to embrace these mindsets – no matter how new and unfamiliar they may feel – will lead you to be more and more comfortable with co-design.

risk–taking and "flearning"

Co-design is an exploratory and iterative process, where we assume that nobody has all the answers. A co-designer needs to be comfortable taking risks, trying things out and seeing what emerges. Many of the best ideas emerge from failures, and knowing what *doesn't* work is crucial to creating a solution that *does* work. We call this "flearning": learning through failure. If you're not prepared to take risks and be wrong, you won't be in a position to innovate.

learning through doing

Co-design, first and foremost, involves action – it's a cycle of creating, evaluating and re-creating. It is not a process driven by talking, but actual doing. It typically involves hands-on designing at the start of the project then testing aspects on an ongoing basis. There should be an emphasis on creating tangible outcomes throughout the entire process, not simply conversations and sharing. This helps to move a project out of "planning paralysis" and ensures that participants play an active role in designing and prototyping solutions.

curiosity

Curiosity is key to navigating the co-design process, ensuring you are open-minded to different perspectives, opportunities and possibilities. The co-designer must be excited to discover new things, leading with a child-like, beginner's mindset that is free of pre-existing agendas, expectations, and prejudices. Curiosity disrupts outdated paradigms, creating space to uncover opportunities for innovation.

optimism

To steer a co-design project through messiness and ambiguity, the co-designer must be optimistic that a solution will emerge. This means trusting the process, courageously leading the team through each design phase, and inspiring trust in others. A "can do" attitude where 'anything is possible' is essential to leading a co-design team through what is likely a new way of approaching things.

embracing ambiguity

Co-design is inherently messy, complex and full of unknowns. You may have to navigate complex relationships between stakeholders, conflicting values and the ambiguity of not knowing what the outcomes of the process will be. A co-designer needs to be comfortable with the uncomfortable, sitting "in the grey" while insights emerge. Cultivating a mindset that's adaptive and responsive, rather than rigid, will allow your team to embrace the messiness as it comes.

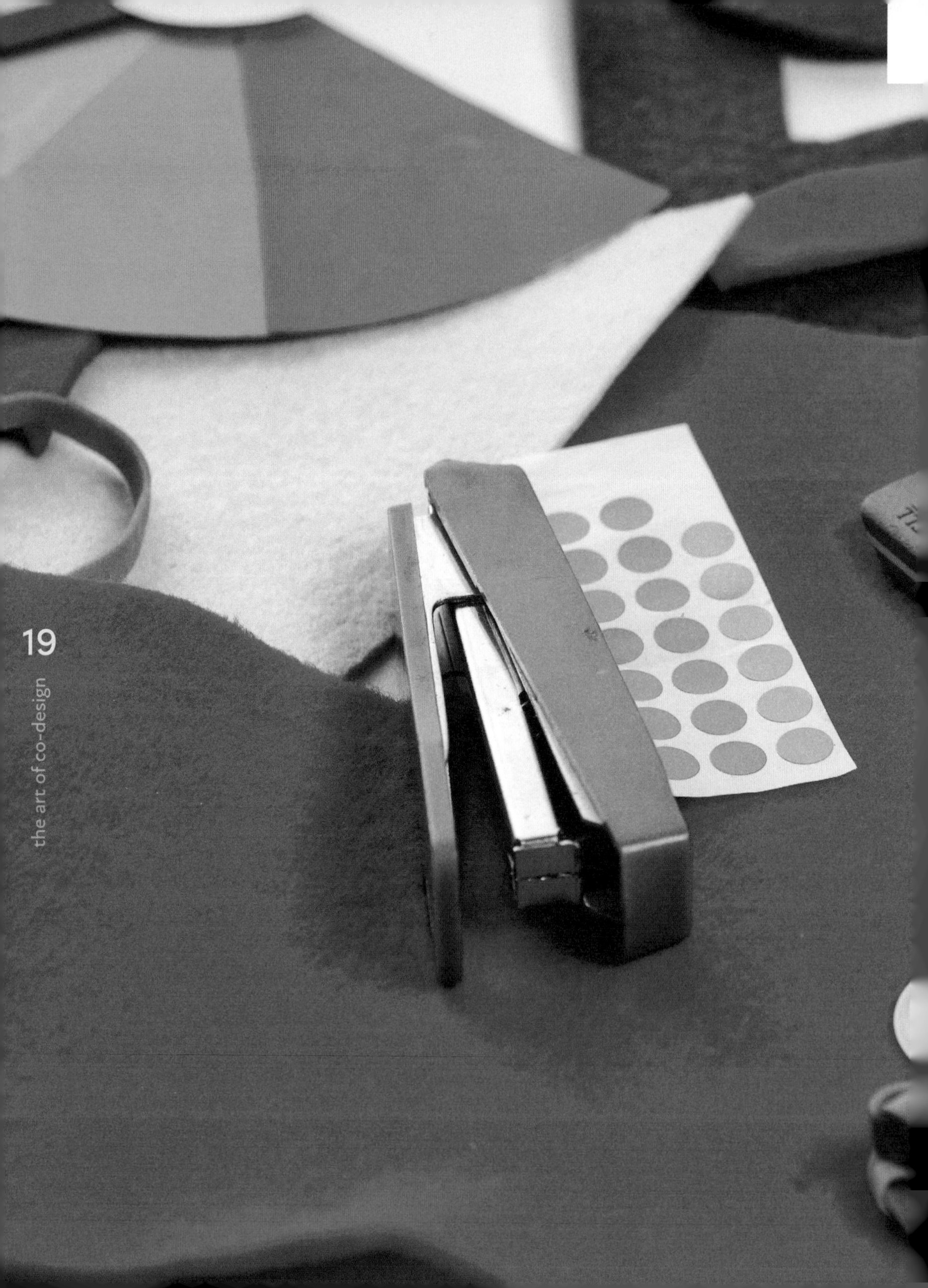

designing for co-design

There are endless creative ways to approach co-design, depending on the context and people involved. Thoughtfully designing the co-design process is equally as important as *doing* co-design, and spending time planning is crucial to effective, authentic and meaningful collaboration. This section will delve into the why, who, when and how of designing for co-design.

step 1

why are you co-designing?

The first step in planning a co-design project is identifying the overarching aim. While co-design is all about collectively defining a design challenge and working to address it, it's important to have a general direction and set of parameters for the project at the outset.

**ask yourself the
following questions:**

what
are the
priorities?

what do
you want to
achieve through
co-design?

what
are the
limitations?

If answers to these questions are relatively prescriptive, the use of co-design may need to be reconsidered. If a solution is pre-defined, this type of complex collaboration is likely to be unnecessary, and instead user-testing and other participatory design methods might be more appropriate. Similarly, if a project requires a quickly-devised solution then co-design may not be appropriate, as it is an extended and involved process, taking longer than standard design. These questions should be revisited with stakeholders after assembling a co-design team.

step 2

who will you co-design with?

Understandably, the key to successful co-design is involving the right people! This not only includes members of the team driving a project, but also the community of stakeholders you will be collaborating with. Identifying the right participants is integral, and takes time and consideration.

building your co-design team

Your team may include:

| subject matter experts | lived experience experts | researchers | facilitators | designers |

Some of your team members might operate in more than one of these roles. Some will be actively involved throughout the whole life of the project, while others may be brought onto the team later in the collaborative process. For example, you may bring on a designer to lead generative co-design workshops and begin to visualise potential solutions, or to design a prototype once the solution has emerged. Through the co-design process you may also identify people with lived experience who have the capacity and interest to be involved with the project at a deeper level, for example co-facilitating workshops, leading kitchen table discussions or co-analysing data.

There are many ways to engage people with lived experience in your project team. While you may not always have capacity or resources to expand your co-design team, bringing a person with lived experience on board from the outset is an excellent way of ensuring a truly collaborative and democratic co-design process. For example, many design settings involve a clear "consumer" or "user" who can be given a defined role (e.g. "consumer representative" or "lived experience expert"), accompanied by a salary, and can work with the team to plan and design the project. Alternatively, it is common practice to create a steering committee or working group made up of stakeholder representatives – both people with lived experience and subject matter experts – prior to project planning, routinely meeting with this group for feedback throughout the life of the project.

identifying your stakeholders

Once you've built your core project team, the next step is to identify the people you will be co-designing with: your stakeholders. There are two main types of stakeholders:

direct stakeholders

people who might use your solution, often referred to as "users" or "consumers"

indirect stakeholders

people who might deliver or engage with your solution on some other level

mapping your stakeholders

We recommend starting by visually mapping your stakeholders by creating a *stakeholder map*. This is a diagram in which you list and rank stakeholder groups, from those most closely involved and impacted by a focus area (typically positioned at the centre of the diagram) to those who are connected (but less so) or influential in the area (positioned further out). The map can be used to identify stakeholders with either lived experience, professional experience or external perspectives that can all inform a project's direction. As a stakeholder map is drafted, you can continually ask yourself "who's missing?" – are there any other stakeholders who should be included? This process not only helps to identify general groups, but potentially groups within groups, including the most marginalised and traditionally under-represented. Other questions that can be asked to identify groups to add include: "who is this for?", "who is affected by this?", "who can influence this?", "who delivers this?" and "who is interested in this?"

Once a stakeholder map is completed, a team can consider the value each person would bring, as well as their need and capacity to participate. This might be impacted by timeframes, budgets and the general feasibility of accessing different groups. A mix of participants with different kinds of knowledge and experience can be beneficial, representing a more inclusive approach to co-design. It's important to engage a diverse range of participants across cultural background, age, socio-economic status, racial background, ability/disability, gender and sexuality.

the art of co-design

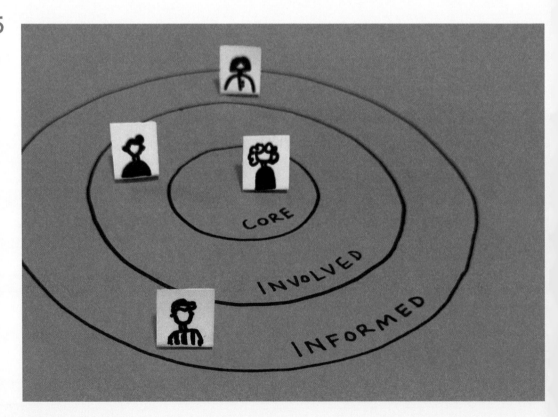

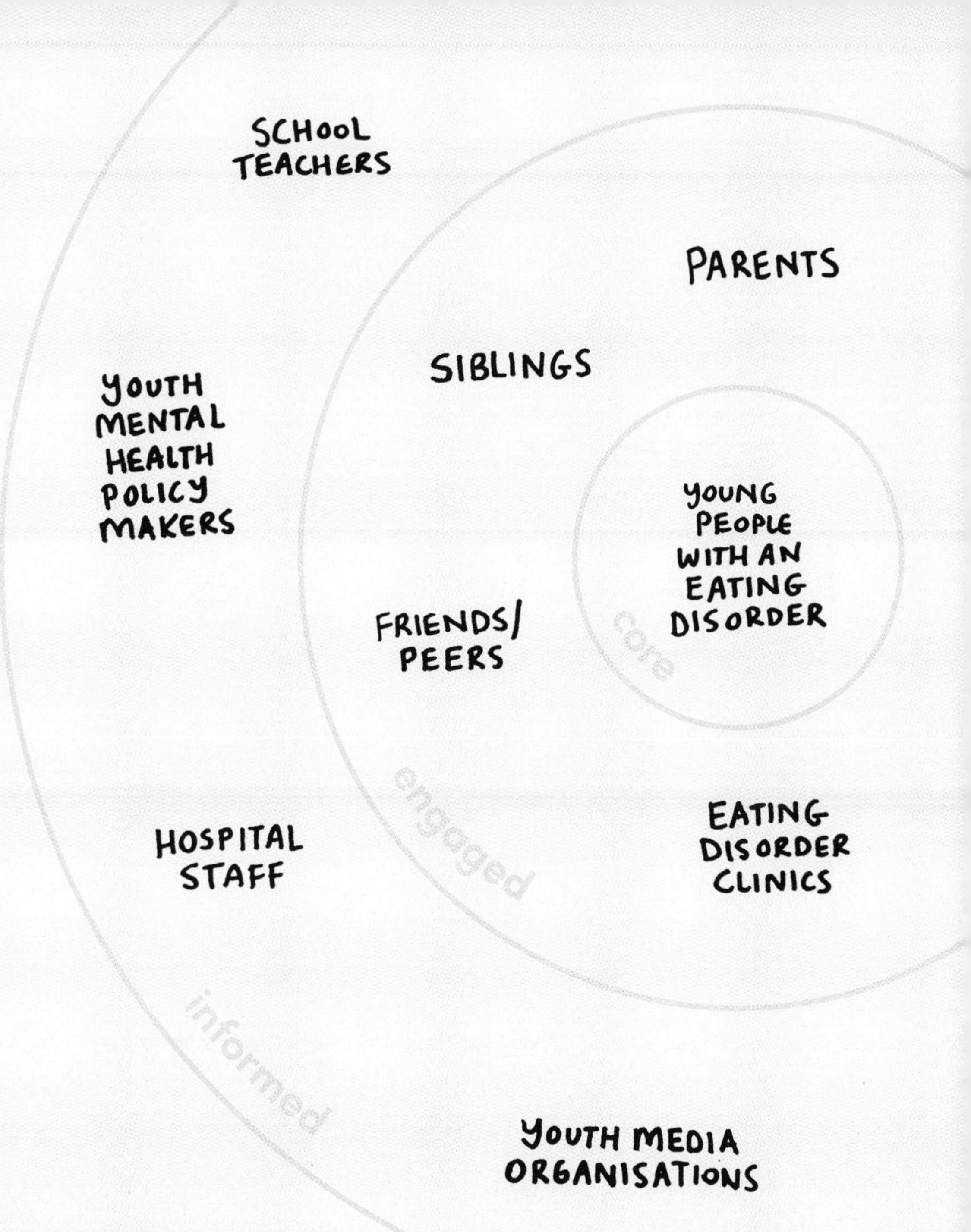

SCHOOL
TEACHERS

PARENTS

SIBLINGS

YOUTH
MENTAL
HEALTH
POLICY
MAKERS

YOUNG
PEOPLE
WITH AN
EATING
DISORDER

core

FRIENDS/
PEERS

engaged

EATING
DISORDER
CLINICS

HOSPITAL
STAFF

informed

YOUTH MEDIA
ORGANISATIONS

Above is an example of a populated
stakeholder map, including potential
participants for a project co-designing
new support services for young
people with an eating disorder.

engaging with specific groups

An additional factor to consider when designing a co-design process is the unique context and abilities of your stakeholder groups, which may require specific engagement strategies. All groups have a right to be involved in a co-design process that centres them, and no one should be excluded because it is "too hard". This section offers some strategies for working with specific groups.

children & youth

When co-designing with children and youth, it is essential that there is no sense of hierarchy; everyone should be treated equally, irrespective of age. Young people should be spoken to directly, especially when parents and caregivers are present, and their input should never be treated as less serious or important than older participants. Methods should be selected and applied in a way that is appropriate and engaging, reflecting the attention spans, cognitive levels and sensibilities of maturing minds. Activities should be explained clearly, avoiding any acronyms or jargon. Create space for flexible, unstructured play, adapting to the interests and attention spans of your participants. Five key principles to consider when co-designing with children and youth are:

Foster a culture of respect for children and youth

Recognise and value the voices of young people

Embrace and appreciate the diversity of children and youth

Create opportunities for storytelling and play

Be flexible throughout and trust in the design process

adult participants with disabilities

As a range of disabilities can impact stakeholder involvement, it is essential that a co-design team identifies the specific needs of participants beforehand. Some disabilities will impact participation in more significant ways than others. For example, participants who are blind will require a redesign of methods that typically rely on sketching, instead reflecting and ideating through conversation. If a person has autism, they may require a stronger emphasis on structure and multi-modal approaches to communicating information, including visuals with verbal direction. Facilitators will also need to understand that neurodistinct participants may differ in motivation and imagination, and may experience a heightened fear of failure compared to participants who are neurotypical. It's important to identify signs of distress from participants during sessions, and to have strategies for minimising distress in place. A series of overarching principles have been developed for *accessible co-design*, which are a good starting point when working with adults with disabilities. These are:

Prioritise the person first, acknowledging disability as secondary

Always use appropriate language that is respectful and inclusive

Approach participants with an offering mindset, never assuming

Allocate additional time to accomodate needs if required

Engage in continuous reflection to improve understanding and practices

Indigenous communities

As a result of historical experiences and government policies, there can be resistance when teams look to co-design with Indigenous communities without appropriate cultural respect. In working with Indigenous communities, it is integral to acknowledge the diversity of culture across these groups, and each must be respected as unique. In recognition of the effects of colonialism on these communities, various approaches have been established which support equal co-design partnerships. These include:

A project should be led, or at a minimum co-led, by someone who identifies as Indigenous

Ideally, at least half of the co-design team should identify as part of the community you are working with

Ensure the process and its outcomes are jointly shared and owned; decision-making throughout a project should occur in partnership

To facilitate community engagement, connect with the people who have established relationships with the community and have them lead this process

Be aware that there may already be events, forums and gatherings to meet with a community, and utilise them

Focus on building relationships first, then co-designing

Come to the community to co-design, rather than working from a team's location

Ensure there is ongoing information provided to the community about progress across a project

CALD participants

CALD is an acronym for Culturally and Linguistically Diverse – a broad-ranging term used to describe communities with diverse languages, ethnic backgrounds, traditions, values, and religions. Within co-design, CALD is often used to reiterate that participants have specific differences that need to be respected and considered, including acknowledging that English is likely to be an additional language. By recognising language barriers and diverse cultural backgrounds, a co-design team can tailor collaborative activities to the needs of participants. Cultural awareness and sensitivity is important, as are practical supports for participants to engage fully. Communication is core to collaboration, and you may need to have an interpreter on-hand throughout the co-design process.

participants with trauma

Trauma may be experienced by many different marginalised stakeholder groups. Because of this, co-design should always be strength-based and trauma-informed. In some cases, participants may have experienced severe trauma and still be recovering from it. This might occur, for example, when undertaking co-design with refugees or people who have been victims of domestic abuse, people with a serious mental health issue, or those who have suffered addiction. In such cases, co-design must be designed to avoid any re-traumatisation and to create an environment in which all participants feel safe. This means that a co-design team must be aware of potential triggers for participants, and have strategies in place for avoiding or mitigating distress.

When collaborating with such a group, facilitators should be clear and transparent about how participants' lived experience will be used and shared. It can be useful to have a trauma-aware mental health clinician as a co-facilitator – this person might not necessarily lead any co-design activities, but would be present to observe any emerging distress in participants and support them if needed. It can also be useful to work with a mental health clinician when designing the co-design experience, ensuring activities are appropriate for your participant group.

people with dementia

While many systems and services are currently being designed to support people with dementia, those people are seldom engaged in co-design due to the perceived complexities. Dementia is often explored through the lens of support workers or relatives, representing an ongoing challenge for co-design: it's seen as easier to engage with indirect stakeholders. This means that direct stakeholders – who the co-design is for – do not have an unmediated voice. Recently, advocates for inclusion have been engaging people with dementia in the collaborative process, with positive impact and innovative results. Key principles that have been applied in co-designing with people with dementia include: focusing on relationship-building prior to co-design sessions, employing visuals and photographs as prompts for discussion, and using informal discussions and engagement. The latter requires a facilitator to be flexible in approach and accommodate the needs and preferences of the participants.

While we have provided some suggestions for collaborating with particular groups of stakeholders, specialist literature exists in all of these areas, which should be reviewed and considered as a co-design project is being designed. The groups outlined above also represent just a handful of potential co-design contexts. In engaging any group of people, especially if no co-design team members identify with that group, you might like to hold an informal meeting with some representatives and run thorugh your co-design plan and approaches prior to the project starting. Use this meeting as an opportunity to iterate and adapt your co-design project to ensure respectful and appropriate approaches.

step 3

when will you co-design?

Once you have an idea of who you are designing with, it's time to consider when you will engage with each stakeholder group. While co-design can occur at any point of a project, as we noted, in an "ideal" co-design process stakeholders will be involved from start to finish. This is seen as best practice, as it results in stronger outcomes and represents a more authentic – and arguably more ethical – co-design partnership.

mapping co-design

A great way of planning your co-design project is by creating what we call an *integrated co-design map*. This is a visual diagram showing the key stages or "meaningful moments" throughout the life of a project, identifying the stakeholders who will be involved at each stage. You can see a basic example of this map below, which can serve as a starting point for you to collaboratively imagine how your co-design process will unfold. Along with being used for initial project planning, it is likely to be developed iteratively over time, and can be used to discuss project planning with the team and stakeholders.

co-design experiences

It is important to plan out all of the collaborative moments along your co-design journey. Your plan will likely change and adapt along the way, but having a general idea of the road ahead will ensure that you are meaningfully and purposefully engaging with participants.

designing for co-design	exploring + ideating	data analysis	prototyping	testing	refining	co-developing	co-implementing

key co-design stages

A typical co-design map will begin with the project planning stage (AKA "designing for co-design"), followed by exploring and ideating (otherwise known as the "fuzzy front-end" – the messy bit), then finally co-developing and co-implementing the solution.

everything that happens in-between

A co-design map should also include everything that happens in between big moments of stakeholder engagement, such as data analysis, developing prototypes, and – if applicable – meeting with a steering committee and informal stakeholder engagements.

integrated
co-design map

the art of co-design

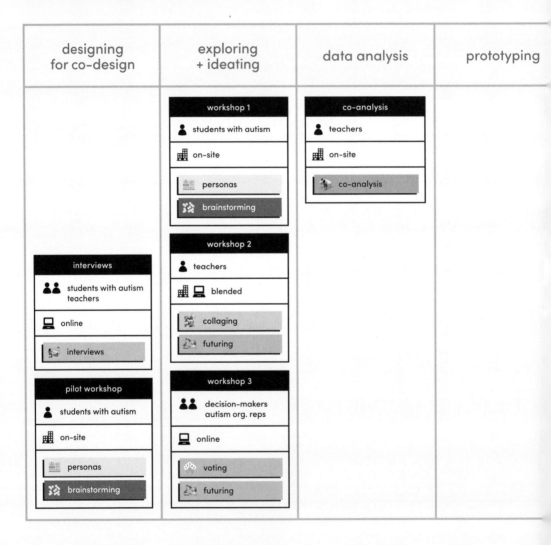

designing for co-design	exploring + ideating	data analysis	prototyping

workshop 1
- 👤 students with autism
- 🏢 on-site
- 📋 personas
- 🧩 brainstorming

co-analysis
- 👤 teachers
- 🏢 on-site
- 🗂 co-analysis

interviews
- 👥 students with autism teachers
- 💻 online
- 🎞 interviews

workshop 2
- 👤 teachers
- 🏢 💻 blended
- 🖼 collaging
- 🔬 futuring

pilot workshop
- 👤 students with autism
- 🏢 on-site
- 📋 personas
- 🧩 brainstorming

workshop 3
- 👥 decision-makers autism org. reps
- 💻 online
- 🗳 voting
- 🔬 futuring

This is an example of a populated integrated co-design map, for a project creating a resource for teachers so they can better support diverse learners in classrooms.

testing	refining	co-developing	co-implementing

user testing 1

teachers

online

think aloud protocol

user testing 2

students with autism

on-site

voting

focus group

resource development

👤 teachers *(national)*

🔄 asynchronous

- - - - - - - - - - - - - - -

working group

👥👤 teachers
decision-makers
autism org. reps

🖥 online

- - - - - - - - - - - - - - -

workshop 4

👤 students with autism

🏢 on-site

- - - - - - - - - - - - - - -

co-design experiences

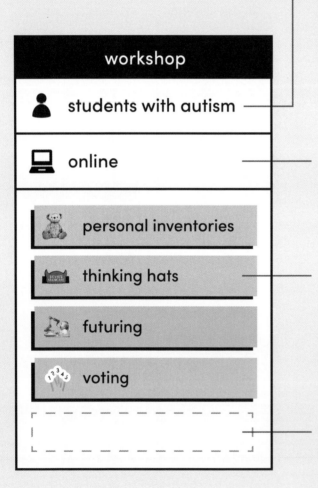

workshop

👤 students with autism

💻 online

personal inventories

thinking hats

futuring

voting

who

It is essential to map the people who you will be engaging with at each stage. Typically, stakeholder groups will be engaged separately in the early stages. However, you may work with mixed stakeholder groups towards the end of the process when you are refining your ideas. The sequence of engagement is important: consider how the insights gained from one stakeholder group will influence the subsequent stages of the co-design process.

where

It's important to consider the format that will be most appropriate for each experience: on-site, online, blended or asynchronous. These formats are explained on *page 37*.

methods

It's important to map out your methods at the start of a co-design process, considering *how* you might engage with each of your stakeholder groups. Jump to *page 39* to learn how to select methods.

unknowns

You may not know all of these details at the start of a project, and that's okay! Leaving space for ambiguity honours the messiness and exploratory nature of co-design, allowing you to listen, learn and adapt to the needs of your stakeholder groups.

35

the art of co-design

tips for making a great co-design map

front-end co-design

Engage multiple stakeholder groups across the front-end of a project, in the earliest stages. Involving diverse stakeholder groups for input and shared decision-making will clarify directions and make sure an idea is fully endorsed as early as possible. It allows for ideas to quickly evolve due to diverse domain expertise, and allows for opposing viewpoints to be reconciled at the beginning of the design process, rather than later.

include mixed methods

As this map is a visual summary of a project, it should include any other research or engagement methods you will be using (i.e. not co-design). This could include large-scale surveys, literature reviews, etc. This allows for the relationship between the components of a project – and how they inform each other – to be clearly considered in planning.

project constraints

In scheduling stakeholder engagement, a team needs to consider resources, budget and timelines. This may mean co-design with stakeholder groups is more limited, but occurs when most necessary across a project. It may also inform formats and methods for co-design chosen in the next steps.

include decision-makers

Decision-makers should be utilised early on to discern whether a direction is viable and should be pursued. Also, just as they can be engaged to identify any barriers to a direction, their expertise can be used to then identify strategies and ways to counteract these barriers.

mixed stakeholder groups

While the involvement of diverse stakeholder groups is encouraged, it is generally recommended that each be engaged separately in the early "front end" phase to avoid issues arising from initial conflicting viewpoints and any perceived hierarchies and power differentials. As a shared vision emerges, mixed stakeholder groups might be engaged to evaluate and refine emerging solutions.

sequencing

Through sequencing, findings and concepts might be generated by one stakeholder group, and then be presented and responded to by a different group, creating an asynchronous form of collaboration (thereby allowing them to work together without the risk of conflict). Sequencing is especially important when wanting to present insights and ideas from one stakeholder group, especially a direct stakeholder group, to indirect stakeholder groups for further development of a project.

iterate your map

The next steps in this section address potential formats for co-design and the selection of co-design methods. These details of a project design can be added to your co-design map, making it an even more comprehensive summary of the project. While a co-design map is made before a project begins, this plan is likely to evolve as a project progresses, and as opportunities arise. It is valuable to continue to add to and iterate the map so it remains an up-to-date "road map" of the project.

step 4

where will you co-design?

Once you have an idea of who you are designing with and when, you can determine what format might be most practical for each co-design stage. Options here include on-site (or in-person) workshops, online and blended workshops, and asyncronous activities. Key considerations here may be location availability, the nature and background of co-design participants, and overall project budget.

on-site workshop

On-site workshops have proven popular because, fundamentally, people are social beings. They allow for a community-driven experience, where informal chats and bonding opportunities emerge naturally. The use of tactile co-design activities can also increase engagement levels. Facilitators can discreetly follow up with participants one-on-one while others work on activities, managing any issues in less confrontational and disruptive ways. Despite their benefits, on-site co-design workshops can be expensive as they may require venue hire, travel expenses for participants and catering.

online workshop

Online co-design workshops are a low-cost alternative to in-person engagement. Ideal for when stakeholders are scattered across different locations or are mentally unable to leave their homes, they create an opportunity to connect with more diverse and marginalised perspectives. Usually, virtual co-design will be held using live streaming platforms (Zoom, Teams, etc.), with the facilitator showing slides and using interactive tools to deliver workshop activities. Some participants may require additional support engaging online, particularly if they have low digital literacy or do not have access to technology or the internet.

blended workshop

Blended co-design is the most complex mode for facilitating co-design, as it involves simultaneous on-site and online facilitation. The facilitator/s are located with on-site participants, with additional participants present online. This presents a set of unique challenges, and activities will need to be designed in a way that is accessible for all participants. This mode is highly flexible and adaptive, allowing for the inclusion of people who can't attend on-site, either due to their location or unforeseen circumstances.

asynchronous activities

Asynchronous co-design does not happen live – instead, participants are sent a series of activities to complete individually in their own time. It allows participants to work around their availability, as well as creating opportunities for unique insights to be captured as participants go about their day-to-day lives. This format can attract people who would not normally be able or willing to collaborate. There are many ways to conduct co-design asynchronously: surveys, videos, written tasks or online feedback tools like Padlets.

step 5

what methods will you use?

Once you have identified the why, who, when and where of co-design, it's time for the fun bit: choosing and designing your methods! There is no limit to the methods you can use or how you can use them. You can simply select from popular and proven methods, adjusting and adapting them to suit your unique projects and people, or even be inspired to invent and design your own. The latter is one of the most exciting aspects of co-design. As co-design is founded on creative methods, there is scope to design entirely new approaches.

using our *A–Z of methods*

To assist you in selecting and adapting co-design methods, we have summarised the most popular methods in our **A-Z of Methods**. Here you will find a short summary of each method, and be shown ways each can vary and be used in different contexts. In most cases, methods can be used for multiple purposes, and don't just have one function. For each method, we've described how they could be used at different stages of the co-design process: *exploring, ideating, creating, testing, sensemaking* and *provoking*. Most of the methods operate on the premise of sketching, making or doing to think, and often inspire a spirit of play. They are designed to prompt people to reflect, hope, dream, make decisions in ways that generate information that is difficult to capture through other methods. This allows participants to *show* a co-design team, not simply tell.

choosing the "right" methods

Typically, a co-designer will look at the **aims** of the co-design, the **types of participants** and what **outcomes** (i.e. data) would be preferable, when shortlisting and selecting methods. While many of the methods we've included are creatively inclined, established methods like surveys, interviews and focus groups can be equally effective and insightful when used in combination with creative methods. While not producing artefacts and designs, they can generate rich discussions and ideas, and they might also be especially appealing to specific stakeholder groups. It is also important to consider the format of the co-design (whether it is to be on-site, online, blended or asyncronous) and whether your selected methods will be appropiate, though many methods are transferable for use across all these contexts. When in doubt, focus on the *people* you are engaging with and the way they feel comfortable engaging. Different methods directly cater for different communication preferences and abilities, which can be invaluable when communicating with diverse stakeholder groups.

collaging	⏱	20 min
bodystorming	⏱	30 min
futuring	⏱	45 min

planning your co-design experience

Once you have an idea of the methods you'd like to use, it's time to piece them together. A standard co-design workshop runs for 1-3 hours, and will include a series of 1-4 linked activities based on different methods. Using a diverse series of methods adds variety and keeps the workshop engaging, giving facilitators the opportunity to pivot if one exercise isn't connecting with participants. This should be considered when planning the final methods selection.

Co-design methods act as building blocks, with the more open-ended and exploratory prompts at the start of the session, and the more challenging and generative exercises towards the end of the session. You might start with methods allowing participants to reflect on their lived experience, then clarify their issues and concerns before designing some initial solutions. Due to time constraints, follow-up workshops may include co-analysing, refining and iterating ideas that emerged from the first session. While this is a practical approach to co-designing a solution, part of the freedom of co-design is that it is not bound by structural "rules", and the design of workshops and the use of methods can be approached in whatever way you think best supports your project.

testing your
co-design experience

If you are uncertain about the co-design experience you've designed, you may want to run a pilot workshop with a small group of stakeholders before engaging with a larger group. A pilot workshop allows you to run through planned activities and receive live feedback for further tweaking. Test participants help refine the workshop for larger groups. Notably, pilot workshops do not involve formal data collection, and are focused on methods and project design. Holding these prior to a project being "locked in" and proceeding, allows any outstanding questions and uncertainties to be addressed and inform the final co-design plan. As well as testing a workshop and its methods to ensure it connects with participants and generates appropriate data, these sessions can be used to discuss and understand stakeholder views and preferences. Engaging participants in this informal co-design context can also assist a team with refining project framing, using an appropriate language and tone, and identiying best approaches for recruiting stakeholders for formal co-design (including the design of recruitment media and scheduling of co-design events).

A-Z of methods

We've collected some of the most popular and effective methods used in co-design to generate a range of outcomes, from exploring and understanding lived experiences to producing innovative ideas and solving complex problems. For each method, we've included an explanation of *what* it is and *why* you might want to use it, as well as ideas for how you could *DIY* the method to suit your specific projects and people.

the art of co-design

affinity mapping

SIMILAR TO:

snowballing
sorting
clustering

what

Organising a large number
of ideas into groups to
identify themes

why

exploring

Clustering insights as
they emerge during
collaborative sessions

ideating

prototyping

testing

sensemaking

Informally clustering
insights or ideas into
groups based on their
similarities

provoking

DIY

There are endless creative ways to adapt *affinity mapping* to suit your projects and people. Here are some of our favourites for inspiration.

collaborative clustering

Low fidelity   **Low cost**

Assemble a group of participants and present a collection of ideas, insights or other pieces of qualitative data that have emerged from the collaborative process. As a group, cluster the items based on similar themes or characteristics.

TIP: *Comparing clusters*

To prompt further discussion, you could allow each participant to go through the clustering process independently, then share their affinity map with the group. This is a great way to ensure there will be consensus in the final collaborative map, and is similar to **co-analysis** in the way that it validates the themes that emerge.

digital clustering

digital clustering

Accessible   Scalable

During a virtual workshop, use an online digital whiteboard tool like Miro or MURAL to document and cluster ideas or experiences into groups based on common features. This is a fantastic way to capture discussions as they're happening and begin the sensemaking process in real time, finding themes and validating them against the experiences of participants.

TIP: *Smooth operator*

Digital whiteboards can be used in two ways: sending a link to participants so they can input their own ideas during the workshop, or selecting one facilitator to be the "scribe" who shares their screen and documents the conversation live. We recommend the latter for participants with lower digital literacy.

snowballing

Low cost   Speedy

Start with a number of key themes, problem areas or ideas written on sticky notes. Continue to build on these topics by adding related items to each, creating a snowball effect as the number of sticky notes multiplies. This is a great way to dig deeper into broad topics, and a fast way of documenting ideas or related experiences.

TIP: *Word association*

A great way to start this process is by using word association – present the first theme and ask each member of the group what words, experiences or ideas first come to mind when they think of this topic.

body storming

SIMILAR TO:
**role-playing
play acting
design games**

what

Acting out how a product or
service would be used

why

exploring

Acting out the current
user experience to
better understand how
the existing product or
service operates

ideating

Acting out how
a current service
could be changed
or improved

prototyping

testing

Testing potential
design solutions by
physically acting
them out

sensemaking

provoking

DIY

There are endless creative ways to adapt **bodystorming** to suit your projects and people. Here are some of our favourites for inspiration.

empathetic bodystorm

Low cost **Low fidelity**

As a member of the project team, imagine you are using the existing product or service, role-playing the user experience. Other project team members might act as service providers or other users, depending on the context. This can help to deepen your empathy towards users, identifying pain points and opportunities in the early stages of the co-design process.

TIP: *Consider location*

If you have access to the location where the experience would naturally occur, you could bodystorm in situ. If not, try using low-fidelity cardboard props to simulate the environment or find a similar location to stage your bodystorming session.

blue sky bodystorm

Low cost **Low fidelity**

Imagine what the ideal, "blue sky" experience of a product or service would be with participants. Simulate or "act out" this experience to better understand how it would look and feel in practice.

TIP: *Prepare props*

If the "blue sky" version of the user experience requires new objects or reconfiguring a space, you can simulate these with low-fidelity components made of materials like paper or cardboard, allowing you to interact with tangible elements in physical space.

scenario storming

Customisable **Low fidelity**

Create a number of different user scenarios based on how the current product or service is used. Act out the current scenario, then act out how these scenarios would change with the envisaged solution.

TIP: *Make it playful*

Consider turning this activity into a **role-playing game** using characters and props. Create an "audience" made up of several participants who can respond to different scenarios in real time.

GOAL CALENDAR

Stress tracker

SPOTIFY PLAYLIST for each emotion

Group gatherings in public spaces

Social media micro content

·ITNESS APPS

regular reminders

DISCORD CHAT

Minecraft game

BOOK LIST

helpline available 24/7

Career Support

Points syste·

CUSTOMIS-ABLE templates

Chat rooms

brain storming

SIMILAR TO:

**idea generation
ideation**

what

Generating and
documenting potential
solutions to a given problem

why

exploring	**ideating**	prototyping
	Generating and documenting ideas in response to a problem or opportunity	

testing	sensemaking	provoking

DIY

There are endless creative ways to adapt *brainstorming* to suit your projects and people. Here are some of our favourites for inspiration.

ten ideas, ten minutes

Low fidelity **Speedy**

Ask participants to come up with ten ideas in ten minutes, drawing or writing down the ideas on a piece of paper. These ideas don't need to be good or viable, as this exercise is designed to get initial ideas flowing rather than to produce ground-breaking solutions. After this process, participants can present one or all of their ideas to the group to prompt further discussion.

TIP: *Evaluating your ideas*

As participants present their ten ideas, it can be useful to give them tools for evaluating them. This could include voting individually or as a group, using one of the solution analysis methods or even clustering similar ideas from the group through affinity mapping.

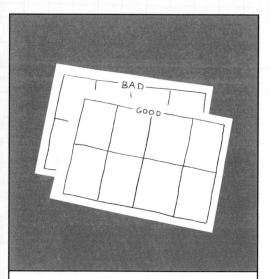

bad and good

Low fidelity **Speedy**

Ask each participant to fold a piece of paper into eight sections. On one side, ask them to write or draw eight bad ideas that respond to a problem or provocation. Then, on the other side, ask them to write or draw eight good ideas. By beginning with bad ideas, participants will start to uncover what characteristics would be inappropriate for the context, and can invert the bad to begin brainstorming the good. It also alleviates the stress of coming up with "good" ideas up front, and adds levity to the brainstorming process.

TIP: *Extra prompts*

If participants are struggling to come up with bad ideas, prompt them to consider ideas that would be inappropriate, use inaccessible technologies, make users more uncomfortable or result in negative outcomes. Following this, ask them to invert their bad ideas, allowing for "blue sky" good ideas beyond the realms of practicality.

structured storming

Playful **Speedy**

Adding structure to the brainstorming process can often spark more innovative ideas – many participants find it challenging to start ideating when the problem itself is too vague. Try using other methods like **personas, extreme characters** and **scenarios** to give the group a clear person or experience they're brainstorming for. You might even use methods like **interaction relabelling** or **conversation cards** to structure this process and provide clear parameters.

TIP: *Set a clear brief*

While structure can support brainstorming, too much rigidity or an overcomplicated and poorly communicated brief can detract from the task. Participants should have access to a clear brief and understand who and what their ideas are responding to.

set intentions	immerse	play	make + test
REFLECTIVE TOOLS	INTERVIEWS	WORKSHOPS	PROTOTYPING
MANIFESTO	STORYTELLING	MAPPING	ROLE PLAYING
	EVALUATION DATA	THEMATIC ANALYSIS	GENERATIVE TOOLS
	PROBE PACKAGES		A/B TESTING

card sorting

SIMILAR TO:

**discussion cards
prompt cards**

Organising or ordering
pre-made cards with words
and/or images

why

exploring

Using cards as prompts
to explore the
relationship between
different words/images,
or asking participants
to generate their own
cards and sort them
by theme

ideating

prototyping

Using cards to
represent components
of a solution, mapping
how they might fit
together

testing

sensemaking

Writing key insights
or ideas from the
collaborative process
onto cards, sorting
them into themes

provoking

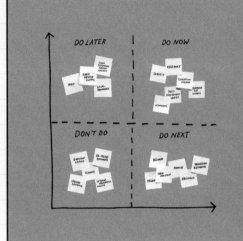

DIY

There are endless creative ways to adapt *card sorting* to suit your projects and people. Here are some of our favourites for inspiration.

priority sorting

Low fidelity **Speedy**

Present participants with a number of cards, each representing an idea or insight. Ask them to sort the cards into an order based on what is most important or relevant to them.

TIP: *Sort again*

To extend on this exercise, try creating multiple prompts and seeing how the order of the cards changes based on the scenario. For example, you could use **thinking hats**, asking participants to imagine themselves as a different person or character and organise the cards from this perspective.

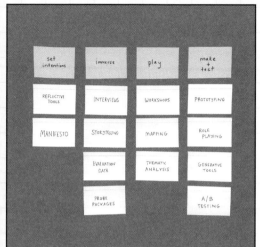

solution sorting

Low fidelity   **Speedy**

When designing a solution – anything from a website to a spatial redesign or instructional PDF – write components of the solution on individual cards and sort them based on where they should appear in the solution. For example, you might sort information into pages of a website, or sort furniture into rooms of a building. Multiple solutions can also be grouped together, representing the holistic consumer experience. This is a great way to start the prototyping process, creating a map of the solution and its components.

TIP: *Make it visual*

Some solutions will be more visual than others, and may lend themselves to drawn elements on cards rather than words. This will make the process more engaging, and it will begin to feel more like a tangible prototype.

task sorting

Low fidelity   **Speedy**

Write a number of tasks or items onto cards and assign them to specific people. These people could be employees of an organisation, stakeholders or members of a family, sorting anything from workplace tasks to household chores. This method can be used in both the *exploring* and *sensemaking* stages of co-design.

TIP: *Change perspectives*

The outcome of task sorting – a map of all of the tasks that need to be completed by each person or organisation – can be used to prompt further discussions. You might sort tasks with users of a service, then take this mapping to service providers and see how they would alter it based on their knowledge and perspective.

co-analysis

SIMILAR TO:

collaborative analysis

what

Collaboratively analysing and
making sense of outcomes from
the co-design process

why

exploring	ideating	prototyping

testing	**sensemaking**	provoking
	Working alongside participants to make sense of everything that you've learned throughout the collaborative process	

DIY

There are endless creative ways to adapt **co-analysis** to suit your projects and people. Here are some of our favourites for inspiration.

the art of co-design

analyse in action

Low fidelity **Speedy**

Begin the co-analysis process *during* a co-design workshop, capturing insights and ideas as they emerge then clustering them into themes.

TIP: *Sticky notes are perfect*

The humble sticky note – whether physical, or digital through a virtual whiteboard like Miro – is a fantastic way to quickly capture and cluster ideas. These can then be taken into a dedicated **co-analysis** session after the workshop and used as data.

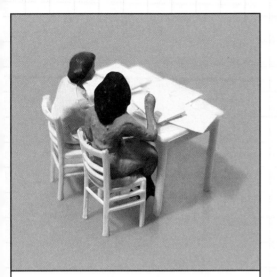

sensemaking together

Low fidelity **Accessible**

After you have collected data through co-design, plan a series of **co-analysis** sessions with one or more participants to identify themes in the data. This may include audio or video footage, written transcripts, written responses, visual responses or even tactile artefacts. You will need to present it in a digestible format without altering or abstracting the data, allowing the group to collaboratively sort individual pieces of data (or "codes") into broader themes.

TIP: *Make it tangible*

Methods like **card sorting** are a fantastic way to view data at a glance when co-analysing in person. Try putting pieces of data – for example, quotes from a workshop transcript – on each card, sorting them into themes.

asynchronous analysis

Low cost **Scalable**

In some instances it may make more sense to co-analyse data asynchronously, with each analyser going through the process of exploring the data and finding themes independently, which can then be compared, contrasted and compiled with the themes of other analysers to arrive at a consensus. This makes it easier for multiple people to analyse the data, and removes any challenges relating to factors like location and time zone.

TIP: *Consistency is key*

You may want to provide instructions or some kind of structure for your analysers, especially for those who haven't been through this process before. Perhaps you could provide a template or spreadsheet for them to fill with codes and themes. A consistent approach will also make it easier to compare and contrast the results.

collaging

SIMILAR TO:

**photomontage
composition**

what

Giving participants a range of visual elements they can combine to create their own image in response to a prompt

why

exploring

Prompting participants to visually depict their feelings or experiences

ideating

prototyping

Bringing ideas to life by collaging design features and elements into potential solutions

testing

sensemaking

provoking

Using collages as a visual provocation, presenting them to stakeholders to prompt discussion

DIY

There are endless creative ways to adapt *collaging* to suit your projects and people. Here are some of our favourites for inspiration.

emotive collaging

Child-friendly   **Playful**

Provide participants with a series of images and image-making tools, before asking them to create a collage that visually represents their emotions around a given topic. This may include open-ended prompts like "what does _____ feel like for you?" After participants have created their collages, you may ask them to label any elements that they feel require further explanation before presenting their collage to the group.

TIP: *Selecting images*

It can be difficult to know how to select images for collaging without leading participants in a particular visual direction. Make sure to include a wealth of different types of images: photographs, icons, illustrations, colours and textures, as well as image-making tools like pens so that they can add their own elements.

utopia and dystopia

Child-friendly **Subversive**

Instead of creating just one collage, ask participants to create two, representing their utopian (good) and dystopian (bad) visions for the future in a given context. Be specific while keeping the prompt open-ended. For example, you might ask them to represent their utopian and dystopian visions for their healthcare in the year 2050.

TIP: *Make it playful*

There are plenty of ways to make this activity more playful and engaging. Perhaps you could play futuristic music as you step participants into a speculative world, use visuals to set the scene, or just playfully introduce the world of the future.

solution collaging

Child-friendly **Playful**

Provide participants with a bunch of different elements that could be included in the final solution. For example, if you were designing a robot you might include different bodies, arms, wheels, a display screen, anthropomorphic features and a host of different possible functions. This is a great way to get participants to prototype tangible solutions without starting with a blank page. It can be done speculatively to prompt discussion, or be used to prototype a real solution.

TIP: *Vary the level of detail*

Make sure to include some elements that are detailed (like photographs) as well as others that are more ambiguous, or provide space for participants to fill in their own details without having to create an element from scratch. Low-fidelity **Prototyping** methods are similar in their use of simple, paper-based elements.

It's opposite day! Introduce yourself to the group, reversing the truth.

Include *your favourite title,*

If your life *theme s* would it

Hum it to *asking the* guess the *s*

Close your and draw a self portrait

Title your masterpiece and present to the group

If your were a course meal, what would it be?

Create a menu describing each dish and present it to the group.

Recreate your favourite place in the world using materials in the box provided.

Ask the group to guess the location.

the story of the items of you're d why

room who knows the least about you, asking them to introduce you.

They will need to guess your favourite meal, hobby and a fun fact about you.

ne up with two hs and a lie about yourself.

Ask the group to guess which is the lie.

conversation cards

SIMILAR TO:

**prompt cards
issue cards
discussion cards**

what

Asking participants to randomly select from a set of cards with questions or prompts for discussion

why

exploring

Exploring lived experience by presenting participants with a set of cards, each with a different question or prompt for discussion

ideating

prototyping

testing

sensemaking

provoking

Using data from the co-design process to create conversation cards with key insights, prompting further discussion

DIY

There are endless creative ways to adapt **conversation cards** to suit your projects and people. Here are some of our favourites for inspiration.

icebreaker cards

Customisable **Playful**

Instead of giving a group of people one icebreaker activity at the start of a workshop, create a deck of cards that include multiple ways a person could introduce themselves, allowing each person to select a card and follow the prompts. This adds an element of surprise to an icebreaker activity, prevents monotony and obliterates power dynamics.

TIP: *Keep it relevant*

Various elements will influence the prompts you include, such as the context of the workshop and the age of participants. In some cases you may want icebreakers to be silly and lighthearted, while in others this activity could reveal nuanced insights that relate to the focus of the session.

public prompt cards

Accessible **Customisable**

Take a deck of cards into a public location that's relevant to your project – for example, a hospital waiting room, park or office – and use images or questions on the cards to prompt short discussions. You might ask people to pick a card and respond to the prompt, or give them a prompt and ask them pick their ideal response from a number of cards laid out on a table.

TIP: *Make it playful*

Consider adding a playful element, like a large novelty die. Participants could roll the dice to land on a question or prompt, then pick cards that best respond to that prompt. For example, you might have a table full of images of parks, with questions on the dice like "which park would you most like to visit?"

metaphor cards

Playful **Subversive**

Create a series of metaphor cards that each describe a different place or object. For example, you may have three cards: library, art gallery and movie theatre. Include information on each card: a title, image, definition and tips for how to connect the metaphor to your problem area. Present participants with one card at a time, asking them "what if [topic] was [metaphor]?" Apply the features of your metaphor to the problem at hand, discussing what you could learn and apply from this seemingly unrelated context.

TIP: *Keep it simple*

Metaphors can be challenging for those who struggle with abstract thinking. Make sure to keep the prompts simple, and include "bridging concepts" or ideas to clearly connect your metaphor with the topic you're exploring.

cultural
probes

SIMILAR TO:

diary studies
journalling
playful probe

what

Cultural probes are documentation tools that are sent to participants so they can capture their day-to-day experiences

why

exploring

Capturing lived experiences when and where they're happening, and creating personal prompts to inspire reflective discussions

ideating

prototyping

testing

sensemaking

provoking

Using visual data and insights collected via the cultural probe to share the story of a person's lived experience with other stakeholders

DIY

There are endless creative ways to adapt *cultural probes* to suit your projects and people. Here are some of our favourites for inspiration.

probe object

Accessible   **Customisable**

Probes don't need to be elaborate packages full of activities! If you want to capture specific details about a person's lived experience as it's happening, make a small probe object that can be placed in a context that's relevant to the experience you want to understand – for example their office desk, fridge or bedroom. This can be super simple and low-cost, with prompts on pieces of paper, or something that's a bit more elaborate and personal. Leave the probe with them for a set period of time, adjusting the activities if needed.

TIP: *Keep it personal*

Add a personal touch to a probe based on something you've learned about the person or people during interviews or initial conversations. This makes the experience more delightful for the person involved, so they are more likely to engage with the probe and find it meaningful.

probe package

Child-friendly   **Playful**

Probe packages include a collection of activities that allow people to document their experiences as they happen. Start by interviewing the recipient(s) to learn more about them and their experiences. Create your package, including items such as diaries, cameras, prompt cards, calendars, stationery and any extra surprises you want to include for the recipient. Provide return instructions, and leave the package with participant(s) for a set period of time. After you receive the returned package, schedule an interview to discuss its contents.

TIP: *Experience design*

Probe packages can be complex, and activities need to be clearly labelled and explained. However, they should also be delightful! Working with a designer can ensure that the package brings joy and curiosity rather than stress and confusion.

playful probe

Playful   **Customisable**

Follow the same process as you would to create a **probe package** or **probe object**, but embed your questions or prompts into a familiar game, such as UNO, Monopoly or Snap. Adapt the rules of the game or replace some of the cards with your own prompts. This works well for groups of people, such as families or co-workers, who may find it easier to discuss serious or dry topics within the context of a game.

TIP: *Keep it simple*

Creating an elaborate game with a long list of rules and complex cards will begin to detract from the conversation at hand, and may make it harder for the group to engage with the questions or prompts. Consider how you can simplify the game so that aspects of it are familiar and intuitive.

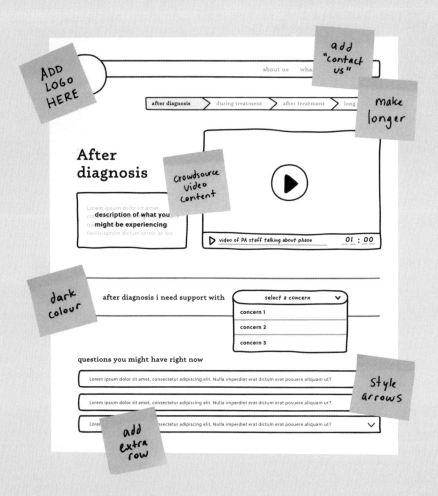

design critique

SIMILAR TO:

design charette

what

Presenting one or multiple design solutions to participants for feedback and iteration

why

exploring	ideating	prototyping

testing

Communicating participants' ideas back to them in a tangible way, exploring whether design solutions accurately represent their needs and iterating further

sensemaking	provoking

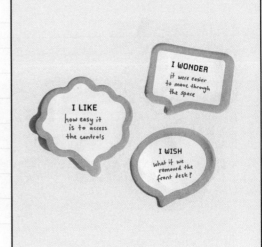

DIY

There are endless creative ways to adapt a **design critique** to suit your projects and people. Here are some of our favourites for inspiration.

i like, i wish, i wonder

Low fidelity   **Speedy**

Present your solution(s) to participants and ask them to respond to the following prompts: "I like...", "I wish..." and "I wonder...". This is a quick, structured approach to getting a read on what participants like about the solution(s), what they are lacking and what other possibilities might exist.

TIP: *Write it down*

As with many other workshop methods, it can be beneficial to write down participants' critiques as they say them, or ask them to complete review cards for each solution prior to explaining their thoughts. This is an important step in validating their ideas and identifying commonalities between responses.

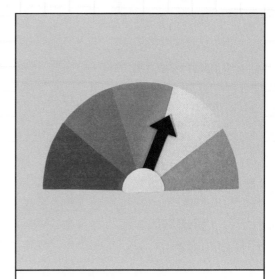

the four "w"s

Low fidelity **Speedy**

Present your solution(s) to participants and ask them to respond to the following prompts: "what is?", "what if?", "what wows?" and "what works?". Prompt them to record their responses on sticky notes, cards or paper templates. This activity will give you a quick snapshot of participants' interpretation of the solution – what they like about it, what they *really* like about it and what other possibilities might exist.

TIP: *Amplify and enact*

Once you have clusters of participant responses to the four W's, you may want to choose one of the prompts and discuss how the responses could be amplified or enacted. For example, you could start with the responses to "what works?", asking what you could do to make these features even better – a "wow".

solution voting

Child-friendly **Playful**

After presenting multiple solutions to participants for critique, ask them to vote on their favourite solution(s). This will give a quick birds-eye view of the preferences of the group. See our **voting** methods for more ideas.

TIP: *Voting categories*

Consider voting based on different categories. For example, participants could vote based on which solution they think is the most usable, exciting, innovative or beautiful. This could be done with coloured stickers, paper gauges or voting paddles for each round.

desktop
walkthrough

SIMILAR TO:

bodystorming
play acting
mock-ups

what

Creating tangible, interactive models of a physical service – either life-sized or a scaled-down "desktop" version – so that participants can "walk through" the imagined service

why

exploring

Creating a small desktop version of the current service and "walking through" it, helping participants to better understand how it functions

ideating

prototyping

Creating a scale model of a proposed service design

testing

Giving participants figurines so they can physically "walk through" a desktop prototype

sensemaking

provoking

DIY

There are endless creative ways to adapt a **desktop walkthrough** to suit your projects and people. Here are some of our favourites for inspiration.

recreate reality

Child-friendly **Customisable**

Create a small desktop version of the current service and "walk through" it, helping participants to better understand how it functions. This works best for spatially-based services – for example, an office or a hospital. You could use a simple image drawn on paper, a cardboard mockup using figurines to act out the function of the space, or something more refined.

TIP: **Compare walkthroughs**

If there are multiple people currently using the service in different ways, ask them to walk through the service individually as they understand it. This can highlight how different people use or operate the same space, providing a more nuanced picture of its current state.

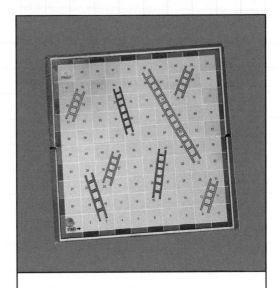

walk through the future

Playful   Low fidelity

Create a model to test and iterate a service that currently doesn't exist. This can be a great way to apply rapid **prototyping**, using simple, low-fidelity tools to make ideas tangible.

TIP: *Tangible materials*

Providing tangible materials like cardboard, pipe cleaners, bottle tops, popsicle sticks and coloured pens can help to prompt playful explorations, encouraging creative thinking as participants prototype their imagined service.

playful walkthrough

Child-friendly   Playful

Combine your desktop walkthrough with a **role-playing game**. This could resemble a board game, or involve action cards that prompt players to consider how the space or service would be used by different characters in different **scenarios**.

TIP: *Meaningful play*

As with all gamified methods, it is important that role-play serves a meaningful role and feels purposeful to participants. Playful methods should add to the level of engagement, prompt participants to consider scenarios that they may not have otherwise and provoke more creative responses.

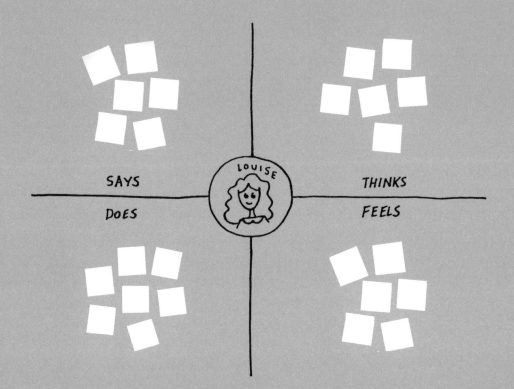

empathy mapping

SIMILAR TO:

saying, doing, feeling, thinking

what

Stepping into the shoes of someone with lived experience, considering what they are saying, doing, feeling and thinking

why

exploring

Creating an empathy map as a team to capture your understanding of the current lived experience and identify areas that need to be explored further

ideating

prototyping

testing

sensemaking

Arranging data from the co-design process into an empathy map that captures nuanced aspects of the human experience

provoking

Presenting the map to other stakeholders to prompt empathy and generate discussion

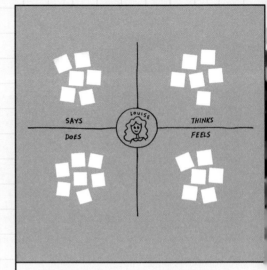

DIY

There are endless creative ways to adapt **empathy mapping** to suit your projects and people. Here are some of our favourites for inspiration.

speculative empathy

Low cost   **Scalable**

To encourage stakeholders to empathise with other perspectives, present them with a detailed persona and ask them to consider what the person says, thinks, does and feels. This exercise is entirely speculative, as it is based purely on the information given about the persona and participant assumptions. However, it is a great way to shift stakeholder mindsets towards the needs and experiences of others during the early stages of the co-design process.

TIP: *Start with what's familiar*

Begin by imagining what the person says and does, as these are more visible and external. If your participants interact with other stakeholders like the persona regularly, these sections will be the easiest for them to complete. They will also create a foundation to explore internal thoughts and emotions.

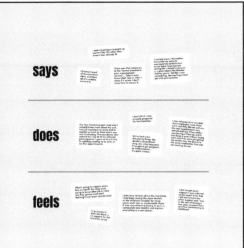

empathy through data

Customisable Scalable

When reviewing large amounts of data as part of the sensemaking process, it can be useful to sort data into different categories to represent the full spectrum of a person's external and internal experiences. Using the same categories as a standard empathy map – says, thinks, does and feels – is a great starting point. However, you can always add your own categories if some of your data belongs elsewhere. This is a great way of sorting data and communicating it to stakeholders, encouraging empathy with another stakeholder's experience.

TIP: *Multimedia mapping*

There's no reason why you need to stick to verbal or written data when creating an empathy map. Consider adding photos of consumer experiences – perhaps using methods like **photovoice** or **mobile diaries** – to add an extra layer of depth to and allow for rich visual storytelling.

self empathy

Speedy Scalable

Ask participants to reflect on their own experiences, documenting what they *said*, *did*, *felt* and were *thinking* in a specified context. This reflective process provides a structure with which participants can explore their experiences in greater depth, allowing more nuanced (and often unexpected) insights to emerge. In particular, aspects of an experience that might not have been considered (like emotions and sensory sensations) can come to light.

TIP: *Support spontaneity*

This activity works best when participants document their initial responses quickly, recording the first things that come to mind before spending more time fleshing out each response. It is important to emphasise responding spontaneously and intuitively, and not to self-edit.

experience mapping

SIMILAR TO:

service blueprint
system mapping

what

Mapping the complete picture of a person's lived experience: any and every action that they might take when interacting with a the product, service or system

why

exploring

Mapping the current or ideal experience from the perspective of different stakeholders

ideating

prototyping

Using an experience map to prototype a potential solution, imagining how the user experience would unfold

testing

sensemaking

Using an experience map to collate and organise different user pathways and experiences

provoking

Presenting visual maps depicting the current experience and ideal experience, provoking discussion around changes that need to be made to achieve the "ideal"

DIY

There are endless creative ways to adapt *experience mapping* to suit your projects and people. Here are some of our favourites for inspiration.

comparative mapping

`Customisable` `Low fidelity`

Ask participants to create two **journey maps**, one of a current experience and one of their ideal future experience, with consistent start and end points. After participants have plotted key events along their journey maps, collate the maps and begin to create a single map that contains each of the possible pathways a consumer could take, turning the **journey maps** into more detailed **experience maps**. Compare the current experience to the proposed future experience, refining the maps to share with other stakeholders.

TIP: *Be wary of templates*

While we recommend using templates to provide structure around an exercise, experience maps can be so specific and complex that adhering to a template can restrict participants' ability to craft a compelling visual narrative. It may be useful to offer some visual cues to participants, while leaving much of the map open-ended.

collaborative mapping

`Customisable` `Low fidelity`

Rather than prompting participants to create individual maps, collaboratively create a single group map that represents multiple perspectives. Provide a base template for the map, prompting participants to add their own insights. This activity is especially effective where representatives from multiple stakeholder groups all contribute to the same map. High-level stakeholders may map their own understanding of a user experience or their service offerings, which can be directly compared alongside "real" user experiences.

TIP: *Add colour*

To make these group maps much easier to read at a glance and identify themes linked to specific stakeholder groups, have participants use different coloured sticky notes. This approach could also be applied to specific themes: for example, blue could represent positive experiences, while red could convey negative moments.

radical mapping

`Playful` `Subversive`

To fully explore an experience (present or future), ask participants to map an *extreme* scenario. This could be an **extreme character** trying to use a product or service, or simply a **scenario** in which everything goes wrong (à la **premortem**). For example, if designing a service for wheelchair users, you could map the day-to-day experience of a user who also happens to be a world champion athlete in an extreme sport. Use these radical maps to reveal "pain points" of an experience, considering solutions to mitigate possible challenges.

TIP: *Serious play*

This can be a very playful and subversive activity to undertake with a group. While it may be fun to explore the most extreme imaginable characters and scenarios, make sure to maintain an element of realism, only mapping experiences that could actually occur.

extreme
characters

SIMILAR TO:

extreme personas
extreme users

what

Instead of trying to represent a realistic target user, design for an "extreme" user with exaggerated traits

why

exploring

Exploring the lived experience of people who sit on the edges of the bell curve

ideating

Brainstorming ideas that would meet the needs of "extreme" users who are poorly represented

prototyping

testing

Testing and evaluating potential solutions based on how well they would address the needs of "extreme" users

sensemaking

Using data from the collaborative process to identify extreme users and their needs

provoking

Presenting extreme user profiles and scenarios as prompts for critical discussion among stakeholders

DIY

There are endless creative ways to adapt *extreme characters* to suit your projects and people. Here are some of our favourites for inspiration.

edges of the bell curve

Playful   Subversive

Look at users of a current or potential service, asking: Who is at the edge of the bell curve? Who are the "extreme" users of the service, or those who are not currently represented? Who are we not talking about? For example, this could be a person with an "extreme" physical disability or a person who does not have access to a phone or computer. Choose a specific user and flesh them out as you would a **persona**, using them alongside personas to ensure that you are designing for *all* users, not just typical ones.

TIP: *Create with consumers*

Consider creating your extreme characters alongside people with lived experience. Being able to speak to actual "extreme characters" would be ideal, however if these voices are inaccessible there is value in exploring these experiences through the lens of other users, helping to reflect the collective needs of the stakeholder group.

just plain extreme

Playful **Subversive**

To encourage creative and innovative thinking during the ideation process, create a **persona** around a character who is just plain extreme. Rather than selecting someone at the edges of the bell curve for your specific product or service, consider someone who is, societally speaking, a generally extreme character: the pope, a fire-breather, an international spy, etc. Then, attempt to design a version of your product or service that would work for this person. Often this process will reveal strange, surprising and innovative ideas.

TIP: *Create space for silliness*

This is an undeniably silly method, which is best used as a warm-up to open participant's minds and subvert their expectations. Creating space for silliness up-front benefits the ideation process tremendously, especially if paired with an artful segue that leads into designing for actual users of the service.

gang of characters

Playful **Subversive**

Instead of focusing on just one character in isolation, create multiple **extreme characters** until you have a group. Consider how this group – or gang – would experience a current or future product or service, discussing whether their needs would be met.

TIP: *All at once*

If appropriate for the project, you could imagine that the gang of characters all access the service at the same time, considering the implications. This is the ultimate test for your solution, leading to unexpected insights and innovations.

focus
groups

what

Gathering a small group of participants to engage in a free-flowing conversation about a chosen topic

why

exploring

Facilitating a discussion with a group of current or potential users to better understand their lived experience

ideating

prototyping

testing

Presenting participants with prototypes of potential solutions, prompting feedback in a structured session

sensemaking

provoking

kitchen table discussion

Accessible **Customisable**

Rather than facilitating a focus group in a controlled setting that is led by a member of the project team, identify a person with lived experience who may be interested in hosting a discussion in their own community, otherwise known as a kitchen table discussion. Provide training, mentoring and support to the host, assisting them to invite participants and prepare discussion questions. Once the kitchen table discussion has taken place, work with the host to evaluate outcomes, perhaps through a process of **co-analysis**.

TIP: *Renumeration and reimbursement*

It is very important to pay participants for their time, especially if they are hosting a kitchen table discussion. Opportunities for renumeration should be clear from the outset, and will depend on the budget and constraints of your project.

DIY

There are endless creative ways to adapt *focus groups* to suit your projects and people. Here are some of our favourites for inspiration.

the art of co-design

two-way focus group

Accessible   **Customisable**

Recruit two groups of participants, including between 4-8 people in each. Facilitate a session with the first group, asking open-ended questions around a given topic. Allow the second group to observe the first group as the discussion is happening (either via a two-way mirror setup, viewing an online session or as quiet observers in the room) or afterwards (by watching a video that you recorded during the session). Facilitate a second focus group with the *observers*, using insights gained from the first session to dive deeper.

TIP: *Two's a crowd*

Be mindful of how a two-way focus group is set up. For example, if the session is virtual, having an additional 4-8 people in a Zoom meeting who aren't contributing may be confusing and overwhelming. Instead, you might record the session and allow the second group to view it afterwards.

yarning circle

Accessible   **Child-friendly**

The use of a yarning circle (or dialogue circle) is an important process within Aboriginal and Torres Strait Islander culture. It encourages honest and respectful interactions between participants, creating a safe space to be heard. Start by sitting in a circle with all participants facing inwards. Invite each person to introduce themselves, before introducing the purpose of the yarning circle. The rest of the session is dedicated to focused questions, allowing participants to take turns reciprocally sharing and learning.

TIP: *Indigenous facilitator*

If you are holding a yarning circle with Indigenous participants, it is important to engage with an Indigenous facilitator who can work closely with the project team to design the session and prepare the focus questions.

forums

SIMILAR TO:

panel discussions

what

Gathering a large group of people to discuss a chosen topic, commencing with a presentation or panel discussion from a group of experts, followed by questions and answers between the "experts" and the audience

why

exploring	ideating	prototyping
Exploring key topics or questions as a group		

testing	sensemaking	provoking
Presenting prototypes to stakeholder groups for critical feedback		

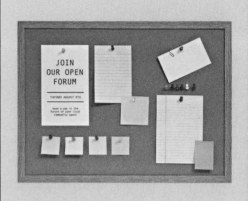

DIY

There are endless creative ways to adapt **forums** to suit your projects and people. Here are some of our favourites for inspiration.

open forum

Scalable **Low digital literacy**

Create an open invitation for your community to attend a forum at a set date, time and location, shared over public platforms like social media. Open the session with a presentation or panel discussion from a group of "experts", followed by questions and answers between the "experts" and the audience.

TIP: *Estimate attendance*

You may want to provide an event link to potential participants so they can register their attendance, allowing you to gauge how many people are likely to attend.

closed forum

Accessible   **Low digital literacy**

Invite a set number of specific participants to a forum discussion, including both users and other stakeholders. As with an open forum, begin the session with a presentation or panel discussion from a group of "experts", followed by questions and answers between the "experts" and the audience.

TIP: _Lived experience experts_

Throughout the co-design process, it is integral to acknowledge users as experts in their own lived experience. It is important to invite one or more lived experience representatives to speak on the panel, chair the session, present the Acknowledgement of Country or shape the proceedings in some way.

bulletin board

Scalable   **Customisable**

If you can't gather participants in person and scheduling a live virtual session is challenging, use an online bulletin board (like a Padlet) to create an asynchronous virtual "forum" in which participants can respond to and discuss a chosen topic. You could include images, text or even videos as prompts, creating comment areas for participants to leave their thoughts. This feedback could be used as the basis for further synchronous discussions.

TIP: _Moderation_

If you are inviting a large number of participants to engage with a virtual bulletin board over a period of time, it is important to review comments regularly to check that participants are understanding and engaging with the content. It is also important to moderate comments, ensuring there are no inappropriate interactions.

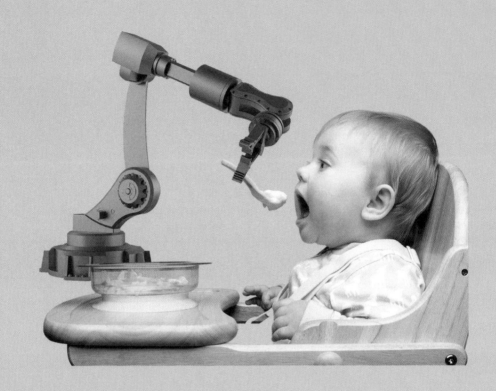

futuring

SIMILAR TO:
design fictions
forecasting
future backcasting

what

Projecting into the future to imagine, predict or dream about how a chosen context will change over time

why

exploring

Imagining ideal futures as a way of better understanding present problems

ideating

Documenting the current situation and ideal future situation, then imagining solutions that would change the current situation to better align with the ideal

prototyping

testing

sensemaking

provoking

Presenting provocative futuristic ideas or artefacts that represent participants' challenges or desires to other stakeholders to spark discussion

DIY

There are endless creative ways to adapt **futuring** to suit your projects and people. Here are some of our favourites for inspiration.

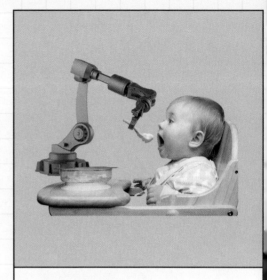

design fiction

Subversive   **Playful**

Design fictions are speculative expressions of potential futures, used to generate discussions and new ideas. They might take the form of short films, provocative **prototypes** (aka **provotypes**) or even graphic novels. You can create a design fiction and present it to participants to spark discussion in a co-design session, or co-design the design fiction itself as a way of expressing the tensions around a topic to other stakeholder groups.

TIP: *Be provocative*

Design fictions may resemble **prototypes**, but they are designed to be subversive, encouraging people to view a topic in a new light. In the process of trying to create a design fiction you might accidentally create a brilliant prototype for a practical solution, which is part of the benefit of exploring ideas in this way.

design forecasting

Customisable **Playful**

Ask participants to project into the future by imagining, predicting or dreaming about how a chosen context will change over time. Give participants one or multiple ways to express their future vision, for example utopian and dystopian **collages**, a **newsflash**, **graphic recording** or just an organic **brainstorming** conversation.

TIP: *Be specific*

Give clear parameters to guide the forecasting activity – a specific year, location, scenario or user. This will help to inspire more creative and nuanced ideas.

future backcasting

Customisable **Low fidelity**

Future backcasting is often done in a "future workshop" format, which has three phases. Begin with a *critique phase*, where participants discuss the current situation in the chosen context. Then, move into the *fantasy phase*, where participants envision the future and come up with ideas to address the problems identified in the previous phase. Finally, end with an *implementation phase*, where participants return back to the present moment and consider what actionable steps can be made towards their ideal future.

TIP: *Mix methods*

A future workshop is a fantastic opportunity to mix methods, using other **futuring** approaches as well as **collaging**, **journey maps**, **brainstorming** exercises, **voting** and many more. Have fun mixing methods in a way that works for your people and projects!

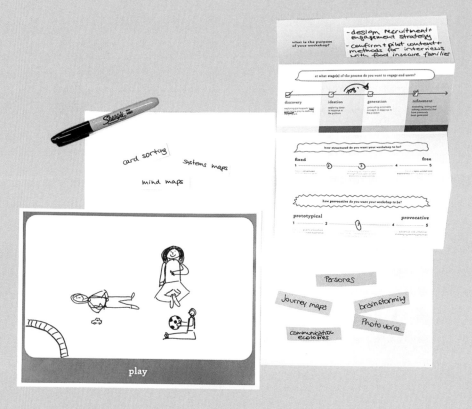

generative toolkits

SIMILAR TO:

tangible making

what

Providing participants with a collection of simple tangible components which they can use to create responses to prompts

why

exploring	ideating	prototyping
Prompting participants to express their experiences in a tangible way using generative tools	Using physical components to document ideas as they emerge	Using generative tools to create low-fidelity prototypes of potential solutions

testing	sensemaking	provoking

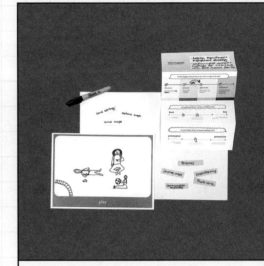

DIY

There are endless creative ways to adapt *generative toolkits* to suit your projects and people. Here are some of our favourites for inspiration.

the art of co-design

make to elaborate

Child-friendly **Low fidelity**

In the exploratory stages of the collaborative process, it can be useful to provide participants with tangible tools through which to explore and convey their lived experience. This could include drawing materials, plasticine, craft materials or anything else that can act as a tool for self-expression. Present participants with these tools, alongside questions and prompts, through which they can tell their story.

TIP: *Quality over quantity*

Providing too many different making tools or options can have the opposite effect – instead of making it easier for participants to express themselves, it may confuse and overwhelm them. Sticking to one main tool per prompt or exercise can be more manageable, and allow participants to focus on the question at hand.

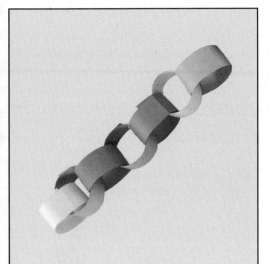

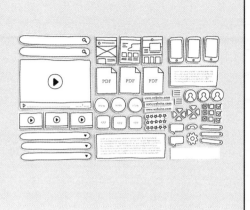

make and icebreak

Child-friendly   **Playful**

If you want to encourage a playful and creative energy from the very start of the workshop, consider opening with a making exercise. This could be a challenge like grouping participants and asking them to make the longest paper chain possible in 5 minutes. Otherwise, they could make something that forms part of their introduction, like a patch representing something they are an "expert" in. Either way, a crafting activity will encourage participants to play and connect, prompting creative thinking.

TIP: *Meaningful play*

Make sure the activity is relevant to the purpose of the workshop in some way. For example, you might prompt participants to craft a personal object that can be used later in the workshop. Alternatively, a creative group activity could communicate the importance of working together, setting the tone for the activities to follow.

prototyping kit

Low fidelity   **Playful**

There are a wealth of different ways to create low-fidelity prototypes that are accessible to all participants regardless of confidence or ability. One way is to create a prototyping kit, including a range of pre-made elements that participants can use to bring their ideas to life. This could include an array of simple generative tools like pen and paper, craft materials, shapes on a computer screen or pre-made solution components. The goal is to create a space where participants feel comfortable tangibly expressing ideas as they emerge.

TIP: *Reuse and recycle*

Prototyping kits can involve a lot of materials, especially if you are working with large groups. We're big advocates of using found or recycled objects (like packaging, fabric/paper scraps or discarded tech components) as part of the prototyping process, as they reduce waste and can often inspire even more novel solutions.

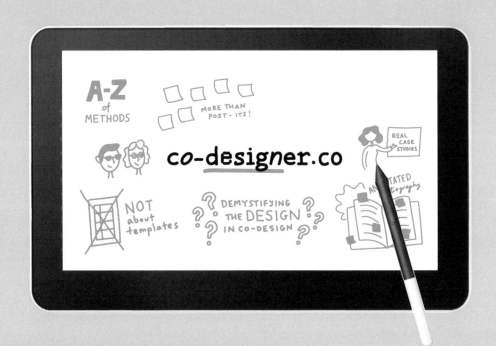

graphic
recording

SIMILAR TO:

reflective graphics
graphic listening
sketchnoting
graphic harvesting

what

Capturing people's ideas and expressions through words and images as they are being spoken

why

exploring

Capturing participants' lived experiences through words and images as they share their story

ideating

prototyping

Documenting ideas and design details visually as they are being discussed, creating an initial prototype

testing

sensemaking

provoking

Presenting a visual representation of participants' ideas and experiences to prompt further discussion

DIY

There are endless creative ways to adapt *graphic recording* to suit your projects and people. Here are some of our favourites for inspiration.

graphic listening

Customisable   **Speedy**

Visually record what is happening during a workshop, interview or other co-design event, then present the outcome back to participants and stakeholders to prompt further reflection around the topics covered.

TIP: *Bring in a professional*

If no-one on the team is confident in their ability to visually document the workshop, there are many illustrators who do graphic recording or "sketchnoting" professionally. Consider hiring an illustrator for the session, leaving you with a higher fidelity visual outcome.

reflective artefact

Customisable   Playful

After conducting workshops, interviews or other co-design activities, create something visual that you can present back to participants to validate and show gratitude for their shared experiences. This could be a storybook, an illustration detailing an aspect of what was discussed in the workshop, or another visual outcome: be creative!

TIP: *Create rich visual data*

By creating a visual artefact for participants, you are also creating something that can be shown to stakeholders as a way of sharing stories, evoking empathy and presenting the ideas that were explored. While this may increase the budget of a project, the impact of sharing tangible outcomes with your community can be profound.

graphic jamming

Playful   Speedy

Encourage participants to collectively contribute to a group drawing in response to a specific prompt. For this visual "jam session", participants could be tasked with capturing an aspect of lived experience or visualising ideas for a design solution. If you feel that participants may be hesitant to engage, or you would like to develop a more refined visual outcome, you could hire an illustrator to act as a visual scribe, bringing to life what the participant group tell them to draw.

TIP: *Creative confidence*

If you are not using a professional illustrator for this activity, emphasise that it is the ideas – not the standard of drawing – that is important. Support people who are not confident in their drawing skills by showing them your own simple stick figure-like drawings and suggesting they annotate anything they think is unclear.

ice-breakers

SIMILAR TO:

relationship building
creative warm-ups
introductions

what

Using a structured activity to introduce participants and co-design facilitators to each other, building rapport

why

exploring	ideating	prototyping
Playfully introducing participants at the start of the co-design process, finding common ground		

testing	sensemaking	provoking

DIY

There are endless creative ways to adapt *icebreakers* to suit your projects and people. Here are some of our favourites for inspiration.

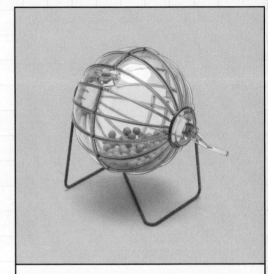

random intro generator

Playful   Subversive

To introduce a playfulness and element of surprise to icebreakers (which can be seen as generic and annoying), write multiple icebreaker prompts on pieces of paper and ask participants to pick one out of a hat/bowl/tombola. Ask each participant to introduce themselves using the random prompt provided.

TIP: *Subvert expectations*

Include a wide variety of exercises, encouraging drawing, role-playing, making, expressing and playfully engaging with other participants. Make sure to include unexpected surprises, subverting participant expectations of the classic "icebreaker" tropes.

diversity bingo

Playful   **Customisable**

Create a bingo card for each participant or group of participants with a number of squares. Within each, write a characteristic that participants might share; for example, "has a tattoo" or "speaks another language". These bingo items could be relevant to the topic at hand or random – whatever works for your project and people. Give participants a set time to go around the room and try to cross off every single item on their card in conversation with other participants. The person or group who cross off the most items wins!

TIP: *Make it achievable*

This is a great icebreaker to use if you already know a little bit about the workshop participants, perhaps through pre-interviews or discussions. You also want to limit the number of bingo items to the number of people in the room or group, so that reaching bingo is achievable.

introducing expertise

Playful   **Subversive**

When introducing participants in a co-design workshop, especially in mixed-stakeholder groups, it is important to be mindful that referencing titles, job descriptions or "expertise" can create a sense of hierarchy in the room. A fun way to subvert the notion of "expertise" is to ask each participant to create and share a patch or other object that represents something unexpected that they are an "expert" in – for example, keeping plants alive or knitting wobbly scarves – acknowledging participants as 360-degree humans.

TIP: *Relevant or random*

Consider if the "expertise" that participants choose should be relevant to the topic of the workshop or entirely silly and random. This will depend on how the icebreaker leads into other activities. Either way, the "expertise" should be something light and unexpected, as opposed to a job title or traditional role.

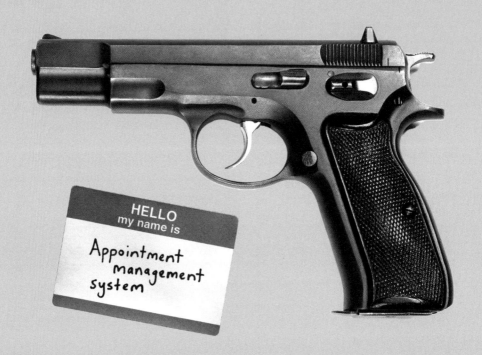

HELLO
my name is

Appointment
management
system

interaction
relabelling

SIMILAR TO:

**product
relabelling**

what

Encouraging new ways of thinking by taking an existing product and pretending it is the product or system to be designed

why

exploring	**ideating**	prototyping
	Prompting divergent thinking by taking an unrelated product and imagining it is the thing you are trying to design	

testing	sensemaking	provoking

conceptual relabelling

Subversive **Customisable**

Pick an existing service or concept to use as a metaphor for what you're designing – something recognisable like a library, gallery or theatre. Present this to participants, asking them to pretend it is the thing to be designed. For example, if designing a hospital ward, present the group with the concept of a library. Consider the functions of a hospital ward, and how these map to a library (e.g. books could represent patients). Continue until all features of a solution (hospital) are mapped to concept (library), discussing what you've learned.

TIP: *Keep it simple*

Activities like this can be challenging for those who struggle with abstract thinking. Make sure to keep the prompts simple, and include "bridging concepts" or suggestions to clearly connect the concept with the solution you're designing.

DIY

There are endless creative ways to adapt *interaction relabelling* to suit your projects and people. Here are some of our favourites for inspiration.

the art of co-design

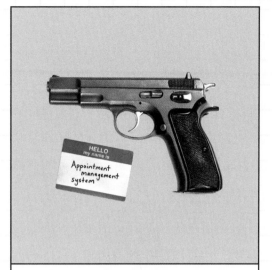

tangible relabelling

Subversive **Playful**

Pick an existing product with some complexity to its functions, something that can be placed in front of participants, such as a tape recorder. Present the object, asking participants to pretend it is the outcome to be designed. What would happen if you had to solve your problem with a tape recorder? What would each of the functions of the tape recorder do? How would they map to the functions required of your solution? Continue the discussion, allowing unexpected, bad and potentially innovative ideas to emerge.

TIP: *Choose wisely*

Make sure to choose an object that has enough features and functions for participants to map their own solution to (depending on the nature of the solution). It's useful to test a number of different objects among the project team prior to the workshop, choosing the one that generates the most interesting discussion.

provocative relabelling

Subversive **Playful**

Pick an unexpected and subversive object that you can place in front of participants. This might be something universally provocative like a toy gun, or something unexpected in the context of your project. Present the object, asking participants to pretend it is the outcome to be designed. What would happen if you had to solve your problem with this object? What would each of the functions of the object do? How would they map to the functions required of your solution? As with *tangible relabeling*, allow ideas to emerge.

TIP: *Read the room*

While the intention behind this method is to surprise and subvert expectations, encouraging divergent thinking, this will work better among some audiences than others. Make sure to read the room!

interviews

SIMILAR TO:
storytelling

what

Having a conversation
with participants about
their lived experience

why

exploring	ideating	prototyping
Asking people to reflect on their lived experience		

testing	sensemaking	provoking

DIY

There are endless creative ways to adapt *interviews* to suit your projects and people. Here are some of our favourites for inspiration.

storytelling

Accessible **Scalable**

Interview participants using minimal prompts. Allow them to freely tell their story and interject only to prompt elaboration. In a group setting this might resemble a *yarning circle*.

TIP: *Create a trigger film*

This kind of open-ended storytelling is perfect to edit into **trigger films**, which can be a great way of ensuring that these valuable stories are shared.

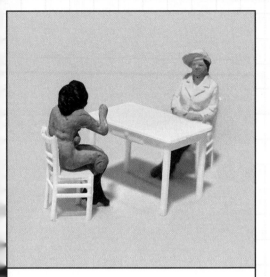

semi-structured

`Accessible`   `Child-friendly`

Plan a series of questions prior to your interview, touching on key topic areas that are important to the project while leaving space for open-ended responses.

TIP: *Learn from others*

As you go through the semi-structured interview process with a range of stakeholders, you will likely want to adapt and expand on your questions based on the insights that emerge. This is a natural and important part of the co-design process, particularly in the early stages.

three whys

`Low fidelity`   `Speedy`

To dig deeper during a storytelling session or interview without asking additional structured questions, you can use a method called the "three whys". When the interviewee speaks to a problem or perspective that you would like them to elaborate on further, respond with "why?", then two more "why?"s until you get to the real root of the problem.

TIP: *Prompt groups to ask why*

This technique can be applied to group settings, particularly when exploring complex problem areas. When the group identify a problem, continually ask "why?" until they reach a satisfying consensus on the root cause.

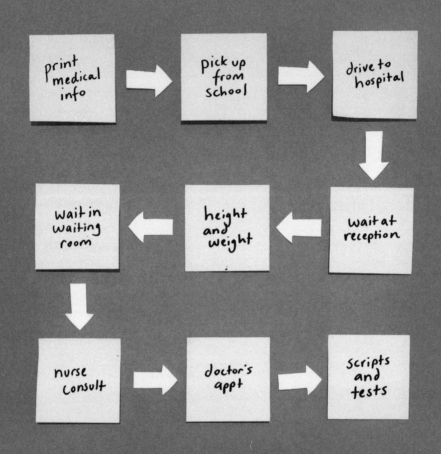

journey mapping

SIMILAR TO:

user journey map
experience mapping

what

Creating a visual story of how a specific person would interact with your product or service in a given scenario

why

exploring

Creating a map of the current user experience to better understand it

ideating

Editing an existing journey map to prompt ideas for how a product or service could be improved

prototyping

Creating a journey map as a prototype that represents the proposed consumer experience

testing

sensemaking

Using a journey map to organise the emotional and physical experiences of consumers

provoking

Presenting a journey map to prompt further discussion among different stakeholder groups

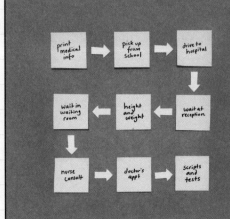

current journey

`Low fidelity`   `Customisable`

Ask participants about a current
experience and have them plot key
moments or tasks across a linear map. It
can be useful to provide a start and end
point, offering some parameters. After
participants have plotted key events,
ask them to add additional layers of
information, such as their feelings, who
they interact with, what technologies they
use and what they need at each stage. A
blank page can be intimidating, so you may
want to prepare a journey map template in
advance, tailored to your context.

TIP: *Provide a visual language*

Beyond creating a template as the basis for
the journey map, you may want to provide
some additional visual directions for
participants. For example, different colours
could represent positive or negative
experiences, and different types of arrows
could represent whether a transition was
smooth or challenging.

DIY

There are endless creative
ways to adapt *journey
mapping* to suit your projects
and people. Here are some of
our favourites for inspiration.

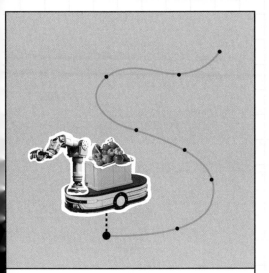

future journey

Low fidelity **Customisable**

When designing a new product or service, ask participants to imagine how it would work in practice, plotting key moments or tasks related to this experience on a linear map. After participants have plotted key events, ask them to add additional layers of information, such as how they want a user to feel and what technologies they are using. After these maps have been created, you may want to refine them digitally so that they are easy to present back to various stakeholder groups for further discussion.

TIP: *Current vs future*

It can be beneficial to create both a current and future map when designing a new product or service, as a way of showing how the user experience would change as a result of the solution.

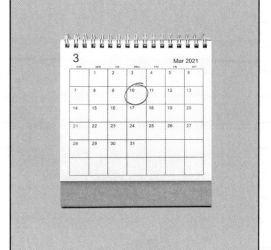

day in the life

Low fidelity **Customisable**

Zoom in on a specific event – whether over the course of a day or a few hours. Follow the same process as you would to create a **current journey** or **future journey**, plotting key events along a linear map and gradually adding additional information around emotions, needs or people. A day in the life map provides an opportunity for added detail – to really capture the nuances of a day and participant routines. You may want to create a template with labelled times across a 24-hour period to scaffold the activity.

TIP: *Visual journeys*

Depending on your participants and their creative confidence, you may want to add a visual element to your journey map, similar to **storyboarding**. While some participants may not feel comfortable drawing, providing the option can result in more detailed and evocative journey maps.

letter writing

SIMILAR TO:

love letters
break up letters

what

Recording your thoughts in an emotive written letter, addressed to a person, organisation, system or personified object

why

exploring

Prompting participants to write a letter to a person, organisation, system or personified object that conveys how they feel towards it

ideating

prototyping

testing

sensemaking

provoking

Reading participants' letters aloud or sending them to relevant stakeholders as a prompt for reflection and further discussion

DIY

There are endless creative ways to adapt *letter writing* to suit your projects and people. Here are some of our favourites for inspiration.

break up/love letter

Low fidelity   **Subversive**

Participants record their thoughts, views and experiences in an emotive break up or love letter (depending on their feelings), addressed to a person, organisation, system or personified object. This context will allow the participant to voice their perspective from a highly emotional point of view, which emphasises positive and negative touchpoints that can inspire the ideation process.

TIP: *Don't hold back!*

Love letters and break-up letters can both bring up a lot of emotions. This activity is a great opportunity for participants to express feelings in an unfiltered way. Emphasise that the purpose of this letter is for participants to let all their feelings out, and they shouldn't hold anything back!

letter to a peer

Scalable **Low fidelity**

Ask participants to write a letter to a
friend or younger peer, perhaps one
who is about to embark on the same
experience they've been through. Tell
them to offer advice and words of support,
considering what they would have wanted
to know. This activity can provoke deep
and thoughtful reflections, and the
opportunity to provide advice and words
of support can inspire ideas that adapt
well to design solutions.

TIP: *Identify a peer*

To make the letter-writing process more
authentic, ask participants to envision a
specific person they are writing to. This
might be a peer they are close with, or
they could create a detailed persona for a
fictional peer prior to writing their letter.

stakeholder pen pal

Scalable **Low fidelity**

Prompt participants to write a more direct
letter to a specific stakeholder who is
relevant to the co-design project. For
example, a consumer could write a letter
to someone who works in service provision
(e.g. a patient writing to their nurse) or vice
versa. This letter can express feedback,
criticism or gratitude for past experiences,
or may involve specific instructions for
how the recipient could best support the
letter-writer in the future.

TIP: *Supporting ideation*

While this activity is great for capturing
lived experience, it can also serve as
a dynamic kick-off or support for an
ideation process. Orienting the letter
towards the future (e.g. "what I need is..")
directly supports the development of
ideas and solutions.

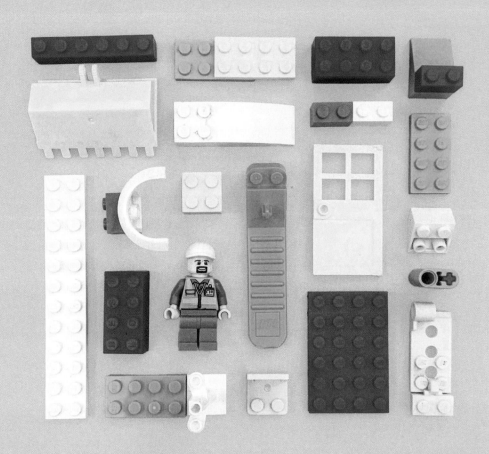

LEGO
serious
play ™

SIMILAR TO:

generative toolkit

what

Making LEGO™ creations in response to questions, acting as a tangible tool to creatively communicate complex ideas

why

exploring

Using LEGO™ blocks as a tool for participants to express and represent aspects of their experience

ideating

prototyping

Mocking up a potential product or service using LEGO™ blocks, allowing the solution to quickly come to life and be iterated on

testing

Using your LEGO™ prototype as the scene for a desktop walkthrough, role-playing how the design would be used

sensemaking

provoking

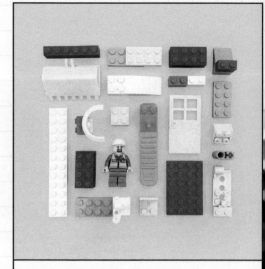

DIY

There are endless creative ways to adapt *LEGO serious play*™ to suit your projects and people. Here are some of our favourites for inspiration.

LEGO™ metaphor

Child-friendly   Playful

Prepare a number of open-ended questions or prompts based on the context, for example, "what does ____ mean to you?" or "how do other people see _____?" Introduce the first prompt to participants, asking them to construct a LEGO™ creation in response. Often participants will use the LEGO™ to construct a visual metaphor or abstract form that conveys their emotions. Ask them to label their LEGO™ creations using sticky notes to clarify key themes and ideas before presenting them to the group.

TIP: *Learn more about LEGO™*

If you're interested in learning more about co-designing with LEGO™, a course is available to become a certified *LEGO™ Serious Play* facilitator.

LEGO™ prototype

Child-friendly **Low fidelity**

Provide participants with LEGO™ in place of other prototyping tools to visualise potential design solutions. You may ask participants to create ideas in response to prompts or scenarios, or simply use LEGO™ bricks as part of your **prototyping** toolkit as ideas emerge in a workshop format. This would work well for a spatial solution like the design of an office or hospital, but it could also be used to design other products and services.

TIP: *Create a desktop walkthrough*

LEGO™ is a fantastic tool to create a **desktop walkthrough**: just add some LEGO™ people and act out how they would move through the space!

asynchronous LEGO™

Accessible **Playful**

Send out a LEGO™ kit as part of a co-design participant pack, providing a list of instructions for what you want recipients to create. After the exercise, ask participants to take a photo of what they have produced and send it to the project team. Along with photo/s, ask them to send you a list of dot point reflections on what they've created and what it means to them.

TIP: *Blended LEGO™ play*

Along with being used for asynchronous co-design, LEGO™ kits can be sent in preparation for a blended or purely online workshop, so that both in-person and virtual participants can play. Online participants can play live, display their creations via streaming software and share details of what they've created.

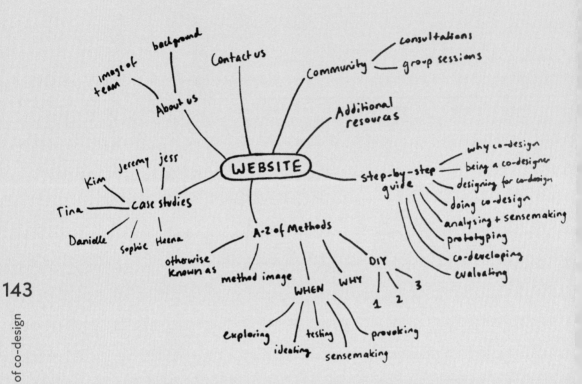

mind-mapping

SIMILAR TO:

concept mapping
spray diagrams
spider diagrams

what

Creating a diagram of key issues or components, drawing links to represent the relationships between them

why

exploring

Visually mapping aspects of a person's lived experience, parts of an organisation or problem areas

ideating

Rapidly capturing ideas and documenting how they relate to each other

prototyping

testing

sensemaking

Mapping data, including problems or solutions areas, to find common threads

provoking

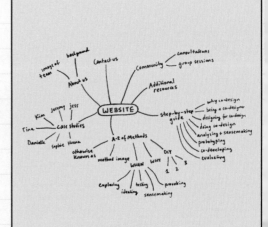

DIY

There are endless creative ways to adapt *mindmapping* to suit your projects and people. Here are some of our favourites for inspiration.

spider map

Low cost   **Speedy**

Pick a central problem or idea, placing it in a circle at the centre of the diagram. Then, think of key themes, features or ideas that relate to the central topic, ideally around 4-6. From here, add an additional layer of detail, branching off into subtopics. Continue to add specificity to your themes and ideas as they get further from the centre of the diagram, adding additional layers that branch off the ones before them. This method can be used when trying to understand a problem space, creating a quick overview of aspects to explore.

TIP: *Mindmapping as graphic recording*

A spider map can be another form of **graphic recording**, with facilitators creating a map as a way of engaging with and capturing a workshop discussion. There is no reason why you can't add drawn elements to a spider map, engaging even more with the spirit of **graphic recording!**

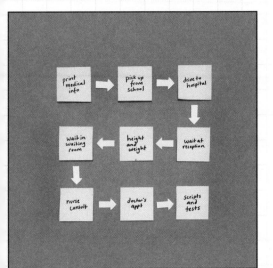

flow map

Low cost   Speedy

Flow maps are used to represent a sequence of events or actions, and are a fantastic tool to visualise a user's experience or the interactions between components of a system. Start with the first step in a process, then map out each subsequent step with arrows between them. You may also want to add sub-steps to provide more detail around what needs to happen in each stage to move onto the next. This can be used to convey the current experience of a product or service, or to imagine an ideal experience.

TIP: *Use tactile tools*

Traditionally all that is needed to create a flow map is a pen and a piece of blank paper. However, using more tactile and movable tools like sticky notes, cards and cut-out arrows can add a layer of playfulness and adaptability, removing the pressure of mapping the sequence correctly the first time and allowing for changes to be made.

circle map

Low cost   Speedy

A circle map is designed to represent varying layers of a problem or topic, and can be adapted based on what is meaningful to your project. Start with a central theme in a circle, then create an additional concentric circle within which you might put sub-themes, key stakeholders, key functions or any features of the theme that are most relevant to you. Continue to create additional concentric circles for extra layers of detail.

TIP: *Make it tangible*

When using any kind of mapping exercise, introducing flexible and tangible 3D elements is a great way to encourage further exploration. For example, if you are creating a **stakeholder map** you might want to draw some icons that represent each stakeholder, or write their names on cards, sorting the cards into relevant sections.

mobile
diaries

SIMILAR TO:

online diaries
mobile ethnographies
video/photo diaries

what

Prompting participants to capture their behaviour over a period of time using mobile technologies like smartphones and low-cost cameras

why

exploring

Giving users the tools to document lived experience as it's happening

ideating

prototyping

testing

Asking users to document their feedback on a potential solution as they test it in their own environment

sensemaking

provoking

DIY

There are endless creative ways to adapt *mobile diaries* to suit your projects and people. Here are some of our favourites for inspiration.

photo/video diary

Scalable **Accessible**

This method is very similar to **photovoice**, in that participants take photos or videos in response to prompts as a way of capturing their experiences in real time. You could supply participants with a camera, however it is generally more accessible and affordable for them to use their existing smartphones. Provide participants with a series of prompts to complete over a period of time. For example, "document your visit to the hospital" or "take a photo of your lunch every day for a week".

TIP: *Consider what else could be captured*

While photos and videos are a great way to capture an experience, mobile diaries can extend beyond this. Participants could record audio, or simply document their emotions in their notes app every time an event occurs.

app diary

Scalable   **Customisable**

There are a number of qualitative research apps that exist for this specific purpose: to provide a platform where participants can upload their responses to prompts, including photos, videos and other creations. They allow you to add your own prompts, which can be delivered at set intervals over a period of time. This approach will cost more than a simple smartphone snap sent over text, but it will provide a more sophisticated, organised approach to data collection and allows you to engage with larger participant groups.

TIP: *Explore your options*

With the demand for qualitative research tools rising, new apps are entering the market regularly. For this reason, we can't recommend a specific app: we suggest you explore and test multiple options before deciding what's right for your project.

reflective diary

Customisable   **Low fidelity**

While photos, videos and digital tools can be effective, some participants may prefer to journal in a more tactile and traditional way. Supply a classic paper diary to each participant, leaving it entirely open-ended, or include personalised notes and pre-written prompts to remind them what to include.

TIP: *Return to sender*

Provide participants with an easy method to return the diary. For example, include a prepaid and pre-addressed package they can slip the diary in and post back to you.

THE DAILY NEWS

VOL. 117, NO. 341

DAILY 50 CENTS

newsflash

SIMILAR TO:
headline

what

Succinctly representing an idea by giving it a "headline", an image and several key points

why

exploring

Communicating a current problem or experience using the format of a newspaper story

ideating

Communicating an idea quickly and succinctly in the format of a newspaper story

prototyping

testing

sensemaking

provoking

Presenting a provocative newspaper story to prompt critical discussion

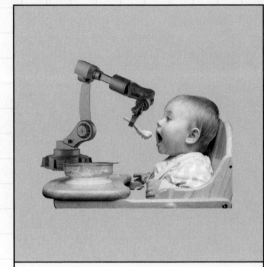

DIY

There are endless creative ways to adapt *newsflash* to suit your projects and people. Here are some of our favourites for inspiration.

forecasting the future

Playful **Speedy**

Ask participants to imagine what their ideal experience or outcomes would be at a given year in the future. Then, ask them to create a newspaper headline for that year which communicates their vision. You might ask them to add an image, as well as a few points detailing the news story. Ask each participant to share their news story, encouraging further discussion. This activity can also be used to explore negative or dystopian visions of the future.

TIP: *Create a template*

This exercise can be completed without a template, however providing participants with a blank newspaper cover with prompts to add text and images adds a level of playfulness and structure, and ensures that all responses follow the same format.

newsworthy ideas

Playful **Speedy**

During the ideation process, when participants are at the point of refining and presenting their ideas, ask them to capture each idea in the form of a catchy headline. They might also include an image and several points relating to key features of the idea. This is a great way to encourage participants to succinctly communicate their ideas and consider the features that are most compelling or "newsworthy".

TIP: *Offer examples*

You may want to provide structured headline templates or examples to prompt participants who are struggling to succinctly communicate their ideas.

paper from the past

Accessible **Speedy**

Ask participants to summarise their past experiences in the form of a newspaper story – for example, "what would be the headline of your life two years ago?" This will help them to quickly explore the central themes of their experience and present their personal narrative. The headline could accompany a drawn image, a photo of their experience or an artefact that embodies the moment in time. Ask participants to present their headline and elaborate on the story behind it.

TIP: *Share your story*

These papers from the past can be a fantastic tool to present the lived experiences of participants to other stakeholder groups. They provide a summary of the key issues that participants are facing, while also conveying them in a highly emotive and evocative voice.

peer jury

SIMILAR TO:

citizen jury

what

Participants are broken into teams who each present an idea in response to a problem. The other participants act as a "jury", scoring ideas against a set of criteria

why

exploring	ideating	prototyping

testing	sensemaking	provoking
Evaluating ideas by presenting them to a "jury" of lived experience experts		

DIY

There are endless creative ways to adapt a **peer jury** to suit your projects and people. Here are some of our favourites for inspiration.

citizens' jury

Accessible **Customisable**

Encourage democratic decision-making by mimicking the style of a "jury". Gather 12-24 diverse, everyday people who will serve as the jury. Bring in "experts" and "witnesses" to give testimonies, before allowing the jury to deliberate as a group and provide recommendations on a given topic. This approach is commonly used by governments to understand citizen perspectives around complex problems.

TIP: *Pre-reading*

As part of the citizens' jury process, it is important to provide participants with information about the topic in advance, giving them time to familiarise themselves. Participants are not expected to be experts on the problem at hand – they are a diverse group of citizens who bring their own experiences and perspectives.

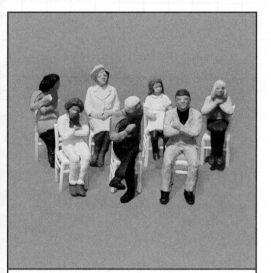

peer jury

Child-friendly **Playful**

During the ideation process, gather a group of stakeholders and break them into smaller groups, tasked with brainstorming potential solutions to the problem at hand. Following this, ask each group to present their ideas, with the other groups acting as a "jury" to evaluate each solution and select the best concept to carry forward into the implementation phase.

TIP: *Cast a vote*

You may want to use *voting* tools to add an additional layer of playfulness and clarity to the evaluation process. For example, you could use physical paddles with numbers written on them, or a digital tool that allows for real-time voting and feedback via participants' smartphones.

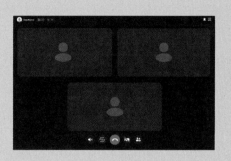

anonymous jury

Accessible **Scalable**

Organise a multi-stakeholder peer jury, hosting the session online. Prior to the event, inform all participants to join with their screens turned off and only interact via chat, so that they are not identifiable. Present ideas to the jury, asking each member to give their verdict via the chat function. After the decision has been made, discuss next steps to move the chosen idea(s) forward. The anonymity of this jury experience can allow for more candid and unfiltered feedback, abolishing any perceived hierarchies in the room.

TIP: *Allow speaking if appropriate*

If stakeholders are not aware of each other (and therefore not able to identify other participants via their voice alone) you can avoid using the live chat function and ask participants to provide feedback verbally.

personal
inventories

SIMILAR TO:

**show and tell
touchstone tours**

what

Using personal artefacts to "show and tell" stories of lived experience and inspire design insights

why

exploring

Asking participants to bring objects from their lives and explore the stories they tell

ideating

prototyping

testing

sensemaking

provoking

Displaying personal artefacts alongside the stories they tell, prompting further reflection and discussion

DIY

There are endless creative ways to adapt *personal inventories* to suit your projects and people. Here are some of our favourites for inspiration.

object as icebreaker

Accessible **Child-friendly**

Prior to a co-design workshop, ask participants to bring an object that's meaningful to them and relates to the topic. If the workshop is virtual, ask participants to find something in their home that responds to a specific prompt. At the start of the workshop, ask participants to present their object as they introduce themselves, explaining its meaning.

TIP: *Set a theme*

Be specific about the kind of object that you want participants to bring. As this is an icebreaker activity, the prompt may be sillier and more informal than a standard **show and tell**, acting as more of a tone-setting exercise than an informative one.

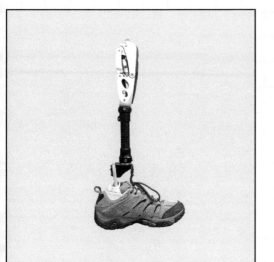

show and tell

Accessible   **Child-friendly**

Prior to your workshop, ask participants to come along with one or multiple specific objects that have meaning to them and relate to an aspect of the topic. If a participant is joining online, they can have it on-hand to refer to. At an appropriate and pertinent point within the workshop, ask participants to share and discuss the object they've chosen.

TIP: *Document the artefacts*

As with all personal inventory activities that involve tangible belongings, make sure all artefacts are documented – typically by photography – during or following the workshop. These images can be included in the project's data and tell a powerful story.

personal gallery

Subversive   **Playful**

After participants have presented their personal objects as part of the co-design process, exhibit them in a gallery setting to other stakeholders and the broader project community. You may present images of the objects, or the objects themselves, depending on their owners' preferences. This is an incredibly powerful and engaging way of telling stories, making lived experience tangible.

TIP: *Annotate the artefacts*

Don't just *show* the personal artefacts – make sure to include a short summary of the meaning and relevance behind each object. This might be constructed using quotes from a workshop or written by the object's owner.

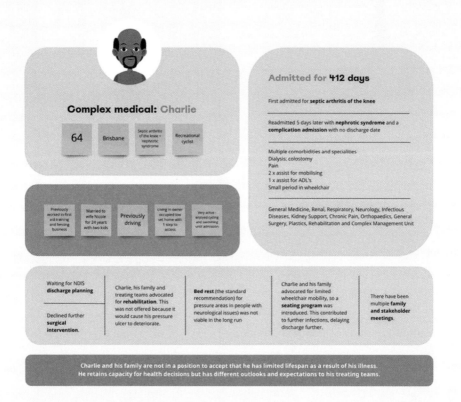

Complex medical: Charlie

| 64 | Brisbane | Septic arthritis of the knee + nephrotic syndrome | Recreational cyclist |

Previously worked in first aid training and fencing business

Married to wife Nicole for 24 years with two kids

Previously driving

Living in owner occupied low set home with 1 step to access

Very active – enjoyed cycling and swimming until admission

Admitted for 412 days

First admitted for **septic arthritis of the knee**

Readmitted 5 days later with **nephrotic syndrome** and a **complication admission** with no discharge date

Multiple comorbidities and specialities
Dialysis: colostomy
Pain
2 x assist for mobilising
1 x assist for ADL's
Small period in wheelchair

General Medicine, Renal, Respiratory, Neurology, Infectious Diseases, Kidney Support, Chronic Pain, Orthopaedics, General Surgery, Plastics, Rehabilitation and Complex Management Unit

Waiting for NDIS **discharge planning**

Declined further **surgical intervention**.

Charlie, his family and treating teams advocated for **rehabilitation**. This was not offered because it would cause his pressure ulcer to deteriorate.

Bed rest (the standard recommendation) for pressure areas in people with neurological issues) was not viable in the long run

Charlie and his family advocated for limited wheelchair mobility, so a **seating program** was introduced. This contributed to further infections, delaying discharge further.

There have been multiple **family and stakeholder meetings**.

Charlie and his family are not in a position to accept that he has limited lifespan as a result of his illness. He retains capacity for health decisions but has different outlooks and expectations to his treating teams.

personas

SIMILAR TO:
user profile

what

Creating a fictional character that represents one of your user groups, including their needs, values and preferences

why

164

exploring

Prompt participants to share their lived experience by identifying with or creating a persona

ideating

Brainstorm ideas that would meet the needs of a given persona

prototyping

testing

Evaluate potential solutions based on how well they would meet the needs of your persona(s)

sensemaking

Create personas to organise user experiences into common themes

provoking

Present personas as a provocation to encourage other stakeholders to imagine users complexly

DIY

There are endless creative ways to adapt *personas* to suit your projects and people. Here are some of our favourites for inspiration.

person to persona

Child-friendly **Customisable**

Work with a person with lived experience to develop a persona based on their story. You may begin with a blank template and add personal details, experiences, needs and desires to the character, or present them with a number of character options so they can choose which resonates most with them. Offer to change their name and personal details when presenting the persona in case they do not wish to be identifiable. Use this persona when ideating potential solutions, evaluating solutions and presenting to other stakeholders.

TIP: *Be trauma-informed*

Personas can serve as part of a trauma-informed co-design process. Participants can create and use a persona that exist outside of themselves – characters who aren't explicitly them, but rather someone with similar life experiences. This allows them to speak to their experiences without having to share personal details.

playing personas

Child-friendly   Playful

When creating or evaluating an idea, personas can be used as a prompt to consider what the best solution might be for a specific person. Ask participants to literally "play" a persona – stepping into their experience and empathising with their needs and desires.

TIP: *Persona hats*

Creating physical **thinking hats** or props is a great way of tangibly introducing a new voice into the room, as well as creating an environment in which it is easier for participants to embody the persona's characteristics.

design by persona

Accessible   Playful

Throughout every stage of the ideation and solution refining process, continually return to your persona(s) and consider if the solution is meeting their needs. Personas may be used with a group of stakeholders as a way of bringing another stakeholder group (such as users) into the room. They can also be used with participants coming from the same stakeholder group, as a more structured way of evaluating solutions based on their needs.

TIP: *Mix methods*

Pairing personas with methods like *voting* can be useful to create a structured frame through which to evaluate if solutions are meeting their needs.

photovoice

SIMILAR TO:
photoelicitation
photochoice

what

Giving participants cameras to document their lived experience, and reflecting on the stories the images tell

why

exploring

Prompting participants to photograph experiences as they're happening, using the images as a basis for reflective discussions

ideating

prototyping

testing

sensemaking

provoking

Sharing photovoice images with other stakeholder groups to encourage discussion and storytelling

DIY

There are endless creative ways to adapt *photovoice* to suit your projects and people. Here are some of our favourites for inspiration.

the art of co-design

smartphone snaps

Accessible **Customisable**

Ask participants to capture their experience using their own smartphones over a set period of time. You might give them prompts or photo ideas, or leave it entirely up to them to decide what's important to capture. At the end of the period, set aside an hour or two in which participants tell the story of each image and why they took it. This could either be as an individual interview or a group workshop.

TIP: *Getting it back*

Make sure to give your participants a straightforward and low-cost method of sending the images back to you, either periodically or at the end of a set period of time. This could simply be by text message, WhatsApp, email or via a platform they're already familiar with.

embracing analogue

Child-friendly   Low digital literacy

Grab a disposable film camera and create a paper cover that gives instructions and photo prompts for participants to capture over a set period of time. At the end of the period, develop the images before setting aside time to present them back to participants and hear their stories. This method is great for children who don't have their own smartphones (although keep in mind they may have never used a film camera before!). It's also fantastic for those with low digital literacy, and offers a more novel experience.

TIP: *Keep it personal*

You may want to interview participants prior to sending out the camera, so you can tailor the prompts to their individual lived experience. This could involve the other people, pets, places and activities in their lives.

snap and tell

Accessible   Subversive

Often images speak louder than words. After you've received all of the photos back and had a chance to sit with participants and hear their stories, exhibiting the images can be an engaging and impactful way to share these stories with the broader community. You can either print the images and plan an event to showcase them, display them for a longer period of time in a context that's relevant to the project, create a website to exhibit them or show them digitally as part of a presentation.

TIP: *Celebrate lo-fi*

Many of the images you receive back might be blurry, low quality or just plain accidental. Celebrate the beauty in real, raw human experiences and display them like art!

the art of co-design

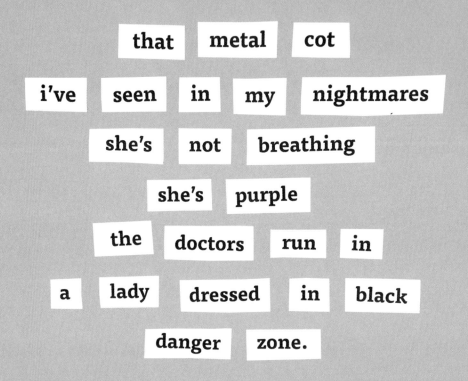

that metal cot

i've seen in my nightmares

she's not breathing

she's purple

the doctors run in

a lady dressed in black

danger zone.

poetic inquiry

SIMILAR TO:

found poetry
poetic transcription
research poetry
data poems

what

Creating poems with participants, or from qualitative interview data, to imaginatively and empathetically convey their unique perspective

why

exploring

Prompting participants to create poems that embody their lived experience

ideating

prototyping

testing

sensemaking

provoking

Creating poems (or poem-like prose) from qualitative interview data and presenting them to stakeholders to prompt empathy and critical discussion

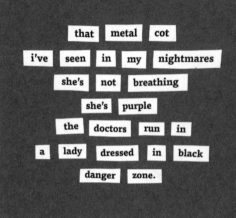

DIY

There are endless creative ways to adapt *poetic inquiry* to suit your projects and people. Here are some of our favourites for inspiration.

data poem

Playful **Subversive**

Transcribe a participant workshop or interview and familiarise yourself with the data, identifying important themes. Choose a topic for your poem based around one of these themes, and begin to highlight text that relates to this topic. Begin to arrange these lines of text to form a narrative in a way that feels true to what was originally said. Remove unnecessary words and refine the poem. Present your poem back to participants for feedback and use it as a storytelling device to encourage empathy among other stakeholders.

TIP: *Poetic license*

Some creative license can be taken with the editing of data – for example, changing the order of words or sentences – to improve the rhythmic structure of the poem. However, it's important to ensure that the emotion and tone feel true to what was originally said, validating this by workshopping the poem with participants.

my friend laura asked me
what happened to your knee
i said
my joints are different now
i have arthritis
oh! my grandma has arthritis!
my heart sank
i imagined myself 100 years old
swollen knees
and cried.

I saw the doctors run in

I heard she's not breathing

I thought danger zone.

participant as poet

Playful **Customisable**

In a workshop setting, encourage participants to write a poem as a way of expressing their lived experience. This poem could take any form – it could involve rhyme, free verse, or be geared towards performance. The goal is to prompt participants to reflect on their own narrative, picking the most salient elements and translating them into a concise but evocative statement of lived experience. These poems can be presented or even performed in front of stakeholders or the general public, encouraging empathy.

TIP: *Provide potential words*

If you anticipate that participants will be stumped when faced with a blank page and the task of writing a poem, consider providing some words that they could **collage** into poetry. You might capture these words during initial discussions or pre-interviews, presenting them back to participants.

fill in the blanks

Playful **Speedy**

Provide participants with a poem template, prompting them to "fill in the blanks" to express their lived experience. The template should include a combination of specific text prompts and blank spaces in which participants can add their own poetic insights. Using prescriptive poetry provokes reflection in a speedy and playful way, reducing the anxiety some participants may feel when confronted with a blank piece of paper and a pen.

TIP: *Use rhyming resources*

The simplest and most familiar poetry format to use is a rhyming poem. To assist with developing a template, you can draw upon online resources that generate rhyming words. Sites like Rhymezone allow you to quickly create rhyming text that can form the skeleton of a prescriptive poem.

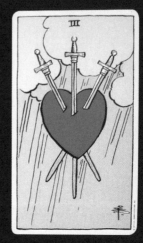

pre-mortem

SIMILAR TO:

postmortem
forecasting
futuring

what

Imagining all of the ways in which a project, product or service could fail, reflecting on the possible explanations for these failings

why

exploring

Before embarking on a project, imagining all of the ways it could fail, then putting strategies in place to avoid these potential pitfalls

ideating

prototyping

testing

After designing a product, service or system, putting it to the test by imagining all of the ways it could fail and why

sensemaking

provoking

DIY

There are endless creative ways to adapt a *premortem* to suit your projects and people. Here are some of our favourites for inspiration.

project premortem

Subversive   **Playful**

To assist with designing a project, the co-design team might begin by imagining all of the things that could go terribly wrong. Work individually or as a group to brainstorm potential problems, worst-case scenarios and premonitions for how things could unravel for the project. This approach may also be used in planning with stakeholder representatives or with participants in early workshops to inform how a project should progress. It allows the team to build a stronger project plan and mitigate fears and apprehensions.

TIP: *Keep it light*

This can be a powerful activity to assist with designing and planning projects. However, it is important that the focus on potential pitfalls does not deflate the optimism people have for the project. Ensure the activity is undertaken in a playful way, laughing at the most ridiculous predictions.

catastrophiser vs optimist

`Subversive` `Playful`

If you are concerned that undertaking a premortem might affect the morale surrounding a project, this activity is a more balanced approach to reflecting on future scenarios: asking participants both "what could go wrong?" and "what could go right?" This could be a two-step process where all participants get the chance to play catastrophiser and optimist, or the group could be divided in two from the outset.

TIP: *One versus the other*

To intensify the playfulness of this activity, pitch the catastrophisers against the optimists, like two teams playing a game. You might like to challenge the optimists to directly solve any issues the catastrophisers raise or vice versa.

solution premortem

`Subversive` `Playful`

A great way to evaluate and test design solutions is to examine them with a stoic lens, expecting things to fall apart. Ask participants to scrutinise concepts and prototypes, looking for obvious (and not so obvious) cracks. Imagine all of the ways that the solution could not work for particular people or in particular scenarios. Use these observations to inform the next iteration of the solution design.

TIP: *Keep it playful*

As with a **project premortem**, it is important to keep the activity playful. Undertake the premortem in a quick and dynamic way, even encouraging the odd outrageous observation that is highly unlikely. If the tone of the discussion become a little too pessimistic, guide the conversation away from that area.

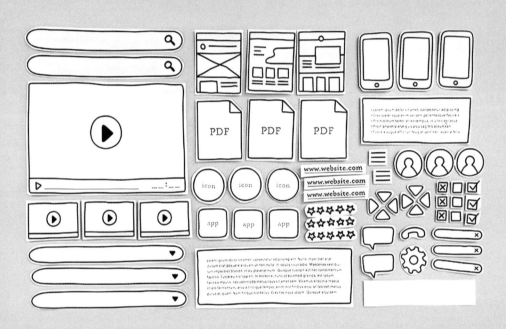

the art of co-design

prototypes

SIMILAR TO:

**mock-ups
wireframing
proof of concept**

what

Creating a rough draft of an
idea, bringing it to life

why

exploring	ideating	**prototyping**
		Creating mock-ups of ideas as they emerge, bringing them to life

testing	sensemaking	**provoking**
Providing prototypes to participants for feedback, iterating on potential solutions		Using prototypes to prompt a broader discussion among diverse stakeholders

DIY

There are endless creative ways to adapt **prototypes** to suit your projects and people. Here are some of our favourites for inspiration.

low fidelity prototype

Speedy **Low cost**

There are a wealth of different ways to create a low-fidelity prototype that's accessible to all participants and facilitators regardless of confidence or ability. When crafting a low-fidelity prototyping session at the beginning of the ideation process, make sure to provide an array of simple generative tools like pens, paper, craft materials or shapes on a computer screen. The goal is to create a space where participants feel comfortable tangibly communicating and iterating on ideas as they emerge.

TIP: *Sans materials*

If you do not have access to generative prototyping tools but want to consider how a solution might look in practice, you could ask participants to use their words and actions to convey the solution, employing methods like **bodystorming** to act it out.

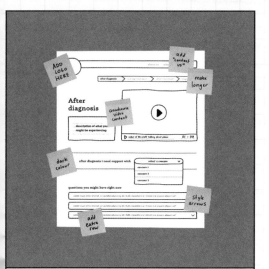

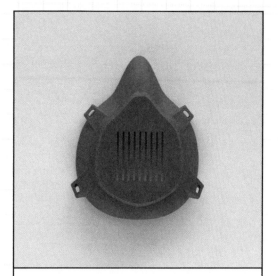

medium fidelity prototype

Customisable   **Playful**

After you have captured initial ideas, you may want to create more advanced prototypes with features that can be directly applied to the final solution. Rather than providing participants with abstract prototyping tools, when looking to create a medium-fidelity prototype you could provide elements that represent specific features of the product or service you're designing.

TIP: *Play with your prototype*

Once you have something that resembles a prototype, you can use this to role play how the product or service might be used, following **bodystorming** techniques.

high fidelity prototype

Customisable

Once you have co-created an initial prototype of a product or service, you will then want to iterate towards a final solution with a series of high-fidelity prototypes. Often this is the stage of the co-design process where a designer is brought onto the team, although ideally the designer has been involved from the beginning. A high fidelity prototype could be anything from an architectural drawing to an initial draft of a paper-based resource or an interactive app prototype.

TIP: *Involve a designer early*

If you anticipate that the outcome of your co-design process will be something that requires the help of a designer – a campaign, app, website, building, etc. – it can be useful to engage a designer early in the process, bringing them along the journey so they can authentically embed collaborative insights into the design.

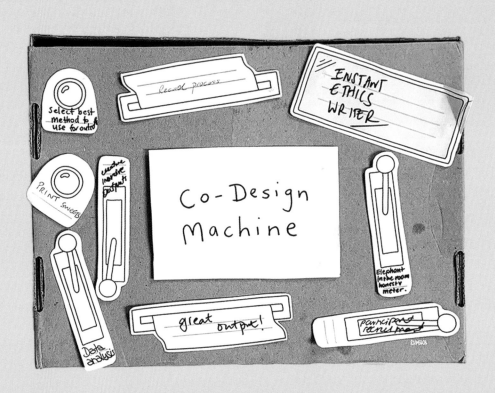

provotypes

SIMILAR TO:

future probe
critical artefact

what

Creating a mock-up of an absurd
or exaggerated design solution,
prompting critical discussion and
creative problem-solving

why

exploring	**ideating**	**prototyping**
	Presenting an absurd or exaggerated idea that prompts creative problem-solving	Developing a provotype into a more realistic prototype that addresses the same problems or themes

testing	sensemaking	**provoking**
		Presenting provotypes to diverse stakeholders and wider audiences to reflect current problems or tensions and invite critical discussion

DIY

There are endless creative ways to adapt **provotypes** to suit your projects and people. Here are some of our favourites for inspiration.

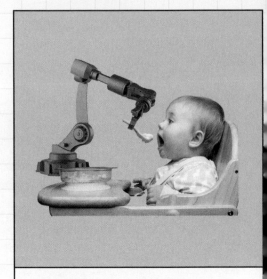

critical artefact

Subversive **Playful**

During the ideation process, present participants with a speculative design solution that subverts their lived experience in some way, prompting critical discussion. For example, if you were exploring solutions to poor nutrition literacy, you could present a concept of a futuristic plate that would scan the nutritional content of the food on it and light up as green (for good) or red (for bad). This could prompt discussions around the ethics of deeming foods "good" or "bad" and having constant access to personal nutrition knowledge.

TIP: *Provotype become prototype*

Typically, critical artefacts begin as low-fidelity ideas – sketches or combinations of images alongside verbal descriptions. However, the level of fidelity may evolve over time. In some cases, the provotype might take on the critiques of participants and evolve into something that is actually implementable.

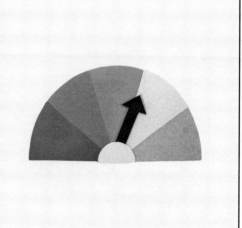

co-created provocation

Subversive **Child-friendly**

In some instances, provotypes can be created *with* participants rather than *for* them. For example, if you want to subvert the current conceptions of service providers around a particular issue, you could work with service users to develop a provocative artefact that challenges the ideas held by those in power. This could come in many forms: a video, illustration or written concept delivered in a compelling way. You might exhibit the artefact and invite many service providers to review it, or use it as a workshop provocation.

TIP: *Provide the right tools*

In the same vein as prototyping, it is important to provide tactile tools for participants to create their own provocative artefacts. They could be in the form of a collage, a poem, a tangible artefact or something else entirely. Encourage creativity!

turn the dial

Subversive **Playful**

Start with a *provotype* or *prototype* and metaphorically "turn the dial". If you have a provotype, consider how you can move it towards a more resolved and practical solution, adjusting elements as appropriate. Alternatively, you may have a prototype and want to make it more subversive and innovative, exploring what unexpected changes could emerge. The act of "turning the dial" in either direction can be undertaken by the co-design team or participants in a workshop.

TIP: *Literally turn the dial*

A way to increase the fun factor and the number of ideas generated is to create a literal spinning dial, which has a spectrum from "extra-wild provotype" to "extremely practical prototype". This could be a Twister-style selector, which randomly lands on a prompt. Aim for at least 3-5 spins of this dial in a workshop.

artist

class clown

skater

role-playing games

SIMILAR TO:

design-by-playing
design games

what

Creating theatrical scenes using simple props to act out and respond to scenarios

why

exploring

Role-playing through familiar scenarios to better understand participant experiences

ideating

prototyping

testing

Presenting a potential solution in a game format, prompting participants to play their way through the experience

sensemaking

provoking

DIY

There are endless creative ways to adapt *role-playing games* to suit your projects and people. Here are some of our favourites for inspiration.

role play in the wild

Accessible   **Customisable**

If the outcome of your co-design project will be a product – for example, a new device, app or tool – give end-users a **prototype** of the future device and observe them as they role play its use in their day-to-day lives. This approach is similar to shadowing in that the goal is to observe them in their natural habitat with as little interference as possible.

TIP: *Create scenarios*

You may want to stage particular **scenarios** in which the product might be used to see how participants respond, rather than following them through long stretches of their daily lives. The degree to which this feels like a "game" for participants is up to you.

interface theatre

Playful   Subversive

If the outcome of your co-design project will have an interface - for example an app or website – **interface theatre** offers a playful environment in which to explore how each component of the system will function. Within a workshop group, assign each participant the role of a different system component (e.g. Marty the menubar), giving them scripted roles to play. Act out a scene based on a specific **scenario**, then adjust the plot based on participant feedback.

TIP: *Props and audience feedback*

It may be useful to set aside some workshop participants to act as audience members, watching the scenarios unfold and providing feedback. You may also want to introduce some low-fidelity props to help immerse participants in the scene, or "costumes" for each character.

character game

Playful   Child-friendly

If you have used **personas** throughout the co-design process, consider creating a game environment in which your personas are the main characters. This could look like a **desktop walkthrough**, in which you create a physical desktop scene that mimics your solution space, or something more abstract. Create scenarios within the game and consider how your characters would respond to each scenario, determining their actions as a group. This is a great way of evaluating potential solutions and exploring new ideas.

TIP: *Tangible touches*

Introduce simple tangible touches, for example image cards or figurines representing each persona that can be moved around the game space. This will make the game experience more engaging and immersive for participants, helping them connect to the characters and their roles.

scenarios

SIMILAR TO:

user scenarios
use cases

what

Describing a number of different situations in which the product or service would be used

why

exploring

Prompting participants to document scenarios in which they currently use a product or service, or would use it in the future

ideating

Using a specific scenario as a prompt for ideation

prototyping

testing

Describing scenarios alongside proposed solutions to communicate when and how they would be used in practice

sensemaking

Analyse data from the collaborative process by finding themes in the form of common scenarios

provoking

Present potential use scenarios to stakeholders to prompt further discussion

DIY

There are endless creative ways to adapt *scenarios* to suit your projects and people. Here are some of our favourites for inspiration.

persona scenarios

Accessible   **Low fidelity**

Present a persona to participants – ideally one that you have co-designed previously – and ask them to brainstorm all of the scenarios in which the persona would use a given product or service. You can repeat this process for multiple personas, building a collection of all possible scenarios for use. These scenarios can be used alongside your personas as a way of evaluating whether products or services will meet the needs of consumers.

TIP: *Keep exploring*

Once you have created a number of scenarios, you may want to select a scenario and incorporate other methods like **bodystorming**, **journey mapping** or **storyboarding** to visualise or act out how this scenario would unfold.

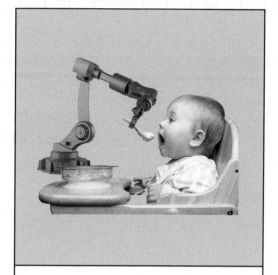

utopia and dystopia

Playful **Subversive**

Ask participants to come up with two scenarios: one representing their utopian (good) vision for the future, and another representing their dystopian (bad) vision for the future in a given context. Be specific while keeping the prompt open-ended – for example, you might choose a specific year in the future. These scenarios can be presented to stakeholders as provocations, or used as part of a **future backcasting** exercise where participants imagine short-term actions that could lead to their utopian scenarios.

TIP: *Mix methods*

You may want to combine this method with other methods like **collaging**, **storyboarding** or **bodystorming** to visualise or act out what the scenario would entail. For example, you might create a dystopian comic strip to storyboard a potential future experience.

scenario as provocation

Playful **Subversive**

Develop a scenario alongside participants, then present it to a different or more diverse group of stakeholders as a prompt for ideation, setting the scene for ideas to come. This could be a scenario that describes their current experience, or it could paint the picture of a utopian or dystopian future. Either way, an element of provocation and subversion is useful when using a scenario to prompt innovative ideation – more unexpected, challenging scenarios will encourage divergent thinking.

TIP: *Novel presentation*

Consider how you could present the scenario in the most evocative and provocative way. You might present it as a **newsflash** or use visuals generated by participants to set the scene. It can also be extremely powerful for consumers to present their own scenarios at the start of an ideation session.

the art of co-design

shadowing

SIMILAR TO:

observation

Following and observing a person
as they use a product or service

why

exploring

Understanding an
existing product or
service by following
and observing people
as they use it

ideating

prototyping

testing

Observing a user as
they engage with a
prototype of a
potential product
or service

sensemaking

provoking

DIY

There are endless creative ways to adapt **shadowing** to suit your projects and people. Here are some of our favourites for inspiration.

in the wild

Accessible   **Customisable**

Observe people as they go about their day-to-day lives in a specific context – whether it's their home, workplace or a third space. You may be trying to understand their current lived experience, or following their use of a new product or service. Either way, the goal is to capture their authentic experience as closely to reality as possible.

TIP: *Create scenarios*

If using shadowing to test a potential solution, you may want to stage particular scenarios, rather than following participants through long stretches of their daily lives. The key here is to avoid creating a sense of artificiality in order to capture the most authentic responses.

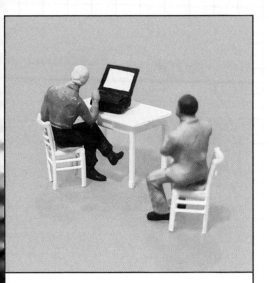

controlled shadowing

Accessible   **Child-friendly**

Ask individual users to test a product or service within a controlled setting, with a facilitator observing as they navigate its functions. This is a great way to gauge immediate reactions to the solution, although the authenticity of the reaction may be somewhat limited if the environment is artificial. You might combine this method with **think aloud protocol** to better understand what participants are thinking.

TIP: *Set the scene*

If shadowing has to occur in a controlled environment like a workshop space or office, it may be useful to introduce elements of the environment in which the product or service would normally be used. It is important to set the scene, encourage familiarity and avoid the uncomfortable feeling of being observed.

work-as-done

Accessible   **Low cost**

Borrowing from safety science, the concept of "work-as-imagined" vs "work-as-done" is useful in any co-design context relating to work. The former describes work that people *think* they are doing, while the latter describes work that people are *actually* doing. Before shadowing people, ask them about the work that they think they are doing, perhaps asking them to create a **journey map** or calculate the number of hours spent doing different tasks. Following this, shadow the same people at work, observing what they actually do.

TIP: *Borrow from other disciplines*

This is a great example of how concepts and frameworks from other disciplines like *safety science* or *human factors* can inspire the way we co-design. Stay curious, and look everywhere for inspiration!

the art of co-design

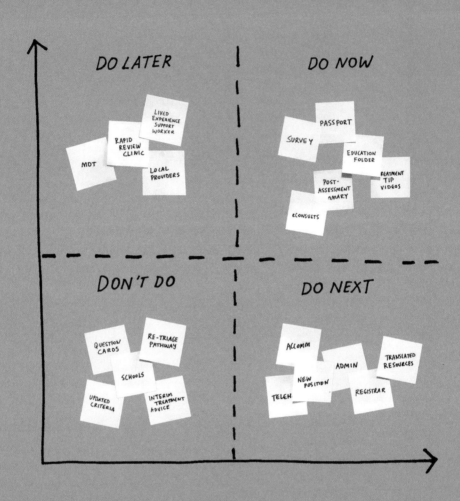

DO LATER

LIVED EXPERIENCE SUPPORT WORKER

RAPID REVIEW CLINIC

MDT

LOCAL PROVIDERS

DO NOW

PASSPORT

SURVEY

EDUCATION FOLDER

TREATMENT TIP VIDEOS

POST-ASSESSMENT SUMMARY

ECONSULTS

DON'T DO

QUESTION CARDS

RE-TRIAGE PATHWAY

SCHOOLS

UPDATED CRITERIA

INTERIM TREATMENT ADVICE

DO NEXT

ACCOMM

NEW POSITION

ADMIN

TRANSLATED RESOURCES

TELEH

REGISTRAR

solution
analysis

SIMILAR TO:

priority mapping
swot analysis
swift analysis

what

Analysing ideas to determine if and when they should be brought to life

why

exploring	ideating	prototyping

testing	**sensemaking**	provoking
	Reviewing all of the ideas generated through the process of ideation and iteration, analysing them to determine which should be realised, when and how	

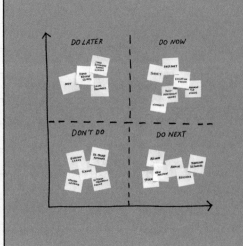

DIY

There are endless creative ways to adapt **solution analysis** to suit your projects and people. Here are some of our favourites for inspiration.

the art of co-design

priority mapping

Low cost **Speedy**

If multiple potential solutions and approaches have emerged from the co-design process, you may want to compare these to determine which should be your top priority. Create a graph with two axes, one representing cost/effort and the other representing impact. Plot your solutions on the graph. One strategy might be to divide the graph into these four sections: low cost and high impact (do now); high cost and high impact (do next); low cost and low impact (do later); high cost and low impact (don't do).

TIP: *Custom labelling*

The way that you label your graph and add meaning to each of the four sections will depend on your project. In some cases, you will be undertaking this exercise to determine which solutions you should and shouldn't implement, while in other cases you will be prioritising solutions that will *all* be implemented.

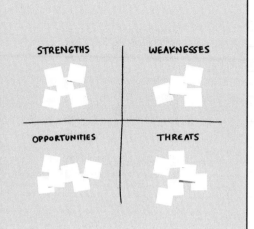

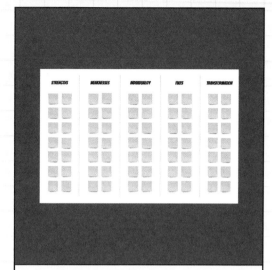

SWOT analysis

Low cost **Speedy**

When evaluating an idea, provide participants with a template that is broken into the following sections: strengths, weaknesses, opportunities and threats. Present the idea, then ask them to note down their thoughts in each section. Compare SWOT analyses to prompt deeper reflections and identify areas for improvement.

TIP: *Make it your own*

SWOT is a common approach to analysing ideas/strategies/organisations, but there's no reason why you can't adjust the wording to suit your projects and people. Words like "threats" may not resonate with some teams – think about how you can make this language your own.

SWIFT analysis

Low cost **Speedy**

When evaluating an idea, provide participants with a template that is broken into the following sections: strengths, weaknesses, individuality (what makes it different), fixes (solutions to the weaknesses) and transformation (changes to be made). Present the idea, then ask participants to note down their thoughts in each section. Compare SWIFT analyses to identify areas for improvement.

TIP: *Analyse in stages*

You may want to take a staged approach to a SWIFT analysis, prompting participants to complete the more straightforward sections like strengths and weaknesses individually, then completing the individuality, fixes and transformation sections as a group.

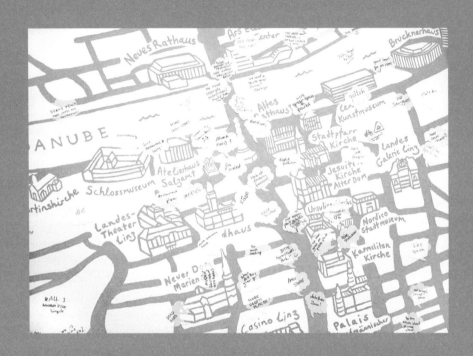

spatial
mapping

SIMILAR TO:

3d reconstruction

Mapping problems or ideas to a
physical location, whether it's a
room or an entire city

exploring	ideating	**prototyping**
Prompting participants to map insights in relation to a physical space		Creating spatial mock-ups of proposed solutions that exist within a physical space

testing	sensemaking	provoking

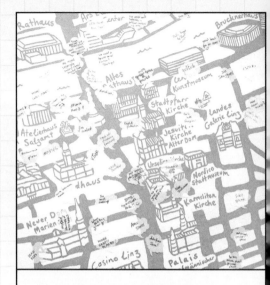

DIY

There are endless creative ways to adapt *spatial mapping* to suit your projects and people. Here are some of our favourites for inspiration.

problem mapping

Customisable **Scalable**

To identify problems or opportunities in a space, city or any spatial environment, create a visual map of the context and encourage as many participants as possible to contribute to the map. Provide participants with sticky notes or other markers, asking them to write one problem or opportunity on each and place it where it belongs on the map.

TIP: *Colour coding*

Consider colour-coding your sticky notes or markers to add an additional layer of meaning. For example, you could assign each participant a different colour, or assign one colour to positives and another to negatives.

desktop mapping

`Child-friendly` `Playful`

When designing a physical space, it is important to begin visually mapping the space as soon as possible. Architects and designers will offer 3D renders and floor plans further down the line. However, there is no reason why this visual mapping can't begin in the hands of co-design participants. Provide your workshop participants with a set of visual tools, such as paper-based room elements. Provide parameters for the design of the space, then allow them to freely imagine potential designs and discuss.

TIP: *Play it out*

To further engage participants in the process of mapping a space, you may want to use methods like a **desktop walkthrough**, using small figures of people in a tiny model of the space to act out how the environment would be used.

mapping in situ

`Low fidelity` `Playful`

When designing within a physical space (for example an office or hospital), ask participants to move around the space and place sticky notes on elements with certain qualities. For example, if you're trying to make the space more playful, put red sticky notes on things that are detracting from playfulness of the space and green sticky notes on the things that are adding to it. This is a great activity to get people moving, and to quickly identify problem areas.

TIP: *Create visual cues*

Using coloured sticky notes or stickers is a great way to highlight salient parts of a room at a glance. For example, if one corner is full of red sticky notes and the rest of the room is green, you know where to focus your attention and discussion. Make sure to take a photo of the sticky notes in situ before removing them!

stakeholder mapping

SIMILAR TO:

ecology mapping
network mapping
ecosystem mapping

what

Identifying everyone who impacts or will be impacted by the project

why

exploring

Identifying each stakeholder group and their needs from the project or potential solution(s)

ideating

prototyping

testing

sensemaking

Identifying how potential solutions might meet the needs of each stakeholder group

provoking

DIY

There are endless creative ways to adapt *stakeholder mapping* to suit your projects and people. Here are some of our favourites for inspiration.

the art of co-design

mapping your people

Low cost **Speedy**

Draw three concentric circles on a piece of paper or whiteboard, labelling them "core", "involved" and "informed" from the centre out. Begin by brainstorming all of the people who will be involved with or affected by your project. Create individual sticky notes, pieces of paper or images for each. Then, as a team, map where each person belongs in your project ecosystem. Mapping allows you to quickly visualise important stakeholders, collaboratively reflecting on their role in the project.

TIP: *Visual recognition*

Prior to a stakeholder mapping session, consider printing out small images of each of your stakeholders (or logos for organisations) to use during the mapping exercise.

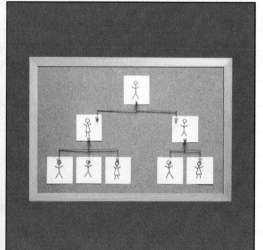

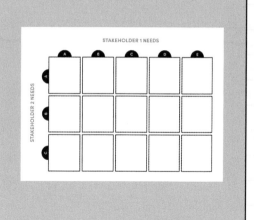

mapping connections

Low cost   **Customisable**

Begin by brainstorming all of the people who will be involved with or affected by your project. Create individual sticky notes, pieces of paper or images for each. As a team, place your people on a desk or whiteboard. Consider how each of these people relate to each other; you could channel your inner detective with red strings and push pins or simply draw connections between them. This will give you a quick birds-eye view of your stakeholders and how they interrelate.

TIP: *Identifying groups*

Before mapping connections, you may want to cluster your people into similar or connected groups. Consider drawing circles around these groups, avoiding the need to draw unnecessary connections between existing teams.

stakeholder comparison

Low cost   **Customisable**

If you have two stakeholder groups with conflicting or overlapping needs, a stakeholder needs table/comparison is a great way to identify opportunities to meet both groups' needs. Create a table with each axis representing the needs of a different stakeholder group. Down one axis, list the needs of Stakeholder 1. Down the other axis, list the needs of Stakeholder 2. Compare the two axes, and look for needs that match, adding a tick. Finally, consider improvement opportunities that could meet these needs.

TIP: *Different perspectives*

Try doing this exercise with multiple stakeholders. For example, you could ask service users to map their own needs as well as the needs of service providers, and vice versa. This will illuminate how one stakeholder perceives the other, and highlight any further sensemaking conversations that need to be had.

story-
boarding

SIMILAR TO:

comic strip

what

Drawing a series of scenes showing how the experience of a product or service would unfold

why

exploring

Documenting participants' current experience through a series of visual images

ideating

Drawing what the ideal experience would look like, presenting it alongside the current experience to generate ideas for change

prototyping

Using a storyboard as a low-fidelity prototype of a proposed solution, showing how it would be used

testing

sensemaking

provoking

Presenting storyboards as a way of generating critical discussion among stakeholders

DIY

There are endless creative ways to adapt *storyboarding* to suit your projects and people. Here are some of our favourites for inspiration.

storyboard as prototype

Child-friendly **Playful**

Prompt participants to draw a storyboard depicting the steps involved in using a product or service. You may provide participants with a blank sheet of paper and pens/pencils, or a template with multiple boxes representing individual steps. These drawings do not need to be sophisticated or even legible to anyone other than the participant – they are a visual tool for understanding how the experience would unfold. If anything is unclear, ask participants to label their drawings and explain them to the group.

TIP: *Refine your storyboard*

After participants have created their initial storyboard, you may want to work with a designer or illustrator to refine the storyboard into something more resolved that can be shown to other stakeholder groups. These illustrations could even sit alongside a journey map, visually depicting each stage.

make a comic

Child-friendly **Playful**

Ask participants to create a comic that conveys a specific experience. This might be their current lived experience or ideal experience – either way, the goal is to tell a story. Provide some examples of comic strips, showing how you can integrate thought bubbles and word balloons to draw attention to specific emotions, people and parts of the story. This is a fantastic method for children, as they can really get creative and emotive when describing their experiences.

TIP: *Pair it with personas*

Comics pair nicely with **personas** as a way of visually elaborating on their story. For example, to create comics with children in a way that is trauma-informed, ask them to create a persona with a similar lived experience to their own, then create a comic that details the experience of this character.

movie of my life

Child-friendly **Playful**

Ask participants to imagine that they are directing a movie in which they are also the main character. Explain that the movie chronicles their experience of a specific event or period of time – whatever is relevant to the topic of the project. Ask them to consider what the key scenes of the movie would be, creating a storyboard by drawing a series of rough sketches in frames, adding a written description of each scene below. Once they have completed their storyboards, they could also physically act out their movies.

TIP: *Make a template*

To make this activity run smoothly, you may want to use a template of a blank movie storyboard. A simple search online will reveal lots of templates you can use, and give ideas for how you could design your own based on your specific needs.

Patient Satistaction Survey

Please provide feedback on your
visit so we can continue to improve your experience

	Very satisfied	Satisfied	Neutral	Unsatisfied	Very unsatisfied
The overall visit	○	✓	○	○	○
The service you received from our staff members	✓	○	○	○	○
The service you received from our reception team	○	✓	○	○	○
The comfort of our waiting areas	○	○	✓	○	○
The comfort of our clinic rooms	○	✓	○	○	○

Tell us how we can improve

it would have been good if we were able to
fill out our appointment questionnaire prior
to the appointment - it's hard to juggle
with a child in the waiting room!

surveys

SIMILAR TO:
questionnaire

what

Providing participants with a list of specific questions to capture demographic information and insights into their lived experience

why

exploring

Creating a survey with specific questions that prompt people to reflect on and share their lived experience

ideating

prototyping

testing

Using a survey as a tool to capture feedback on a potential solution

sensemaking

provoking

DIY

There are endless creative ways to adapt **surveys** to suit your projects and people. Here are some of our favourites for inspiration.

closed survey

Scalable **Speedy**

If your goal is to quickly capture a wealth of numerical data from a large number of participants, a closed (or quantitative) survey is the way to go. Create a survey with multiple choice, yes/no or agree/ disagree answers and distribute it to participants either physically or digitally.

TIP: _Try survey software_

There are plenty of existing online survey-making tools that can improve the experience for users. Take advantage of these tools; many of them are free to use!

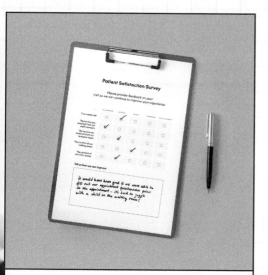

open survey

Scalable **Accessible**

If your goal is to capture more nuanced responses that represent the experiences of a large number of participants, a more open (or qualitative) survey is the way to go. Create a physical or virtual survey with text fields that allow participants to input their own written responses. Depending on the kind of information you're hoping to capture, you may want to offer a mix of closed and open-ended questions.

TIP: *Offer examples*

It can be useful to provide some brief examples of the kind of responses you're hoping to receive for each question, or add additional prompts so respondents understand how to answer. Be careful not to include anything too specific that might lead the tone or direction of their response so that it is no longer authentic.

mixed media survey

Playful **Customisable**

If you want to capture the experiences of a large or small number of people in a rich and playful way, consider creating a multimedia survey that includes a range of qualitative, quantitative and visually rich prompts. You could include photos or videos as prompts, or consider creative ways for participants to submit their own responses.

TIP: *Simple may be best*

While it is tempting to explore playful approaches to capturing data, it is possible for prompts and questions to get lost in translation if the project team are not present while they are being completed. To counter this, begin with simple multiple choice questions and open-ended text fields before introducing more creative prompts.

think aloud protocol

SIMILAR TO:

**thinking aloud
thought verbalising**

what

Asking participants to "think aloud" or explain their thought process as they perform a set of specified tasks

why

exploring

Audio recording people's thoughts as they go through an experience

ideating	prototyping

testing

Documenting feedback by asking participants to record their thoughts as they use a prototype

sensemaking	provoking

DIY

There are endless creative ways to adapt *think aloud protocol* to suit your projects and people. Here are some of our favourites for inspiration.

home recording

Scalable   **Accessible**

Ask participants to record audio or video of themselves as they use your product or service in their home environments. This is an excellent way of capturing authentic responses to a potential solution in the environment where it is most commonly used.

TIP: *Easy returns*

Make sure that participants are clear on how to send the recordings to you, especially if the files might be quite large. There are qualitative research websites and apps that allow participants to upload audio and video recordings in response to set prompts, which may be worth exploring for larger groups of participants.

think aloud testing

Child-friendly **Speedy**

Ask individual participants to test a product or service in a controlled setting, thinking aloud as they navigate its functions, with a facilitator observing the testing session. This is a great way to gauge immediate reactions to the solution, although the authenticity of the reaction may be somewhat limited if the environment is artificial.

TIP: *Set the scene*

If think aloud testing has to occur in a controlled environment like a workshop space or office, it may be useful to introduce elements of the environment in which the product or service would normally be used. Set the scene, add familiarity and try to detract from the uncomfortable feeling of being observed.

wizard of oz

Playful **Customisable**

Create a low or medium fidelity prototype of a product or service where a facilitator can operate behind-the-scenes to create the illusion that the prototype is working and responding to the actions and inputs of participants. For example, your "wizard of oz" facilitator could make sounds, move components or describe what would happen based on the input given. This is a fun and engaging way to evaluate the functionality of a solution before committing to a high-fidelity prototype.

TIP: *Behind the curtain*

While participants may be privy to the fact that responses are human-generated, it can be even more effective if you are able to simulate the interaction without "breaking the fourth wall" and revealing the wizard behind the curtain.

thinking hats

SIMILAR TO:

persona hats
character hats

what

Using hats to represent different perspectives, inviting participants to "wear" the hat – either physically or metaphorically – when reflecting on a given topic

why

exploring

Taking turns adopting different physical hats that represent key perspectives that need to be understood

ideating

Adopting different perspectives to encourage creative thinking while coming up with ideas

prototyping

testing

Providing feedback on potential solutions while playing a specific character or person, imagining how they would respond

sensemaking

Adopting alternate perspectives when analysing insights and learnings

provoking

DIY

There are endless creative ways to adapt *thinking hats* to suit your projects and people. Here are some of our favourites for inspiration.

the devil's advocate

Playful   Subversive

When evaluating ideas, it can be useful to create a safe space for participants to adopt more provocative and subversive roles. For example, if there is a power dynamic or sense of conflict among a group of stakeholders, actively encouraging a member of the group to play "devil's advocate" in a safe and structured way can allow critical discussions to emerge. Create a physical hat, asking one person to wear the hat and adopt the mindset of the devil's advocate or other character when critiquing ideas.

TIP: *Introduce multiple hats*

Depending on the context, it may be useful to introduce multiple different hats to explore the positives, negatives and opportunities surrounding each idea: for example, the "optimist" or "curious child".

pair with personas

Playful   **Customisable**

If you have used **personas** throughout the co-design process, an excellent way of "bringing them into the room" when ideas are being evaluated is to create visual props like thinking hats. Assign the hat to a person in the room whose task it is to view and respond to all matters through the eyes of the persona. You might do this with one or multiple personas within the same session.

TIP: *Pass the hat around*

It can be useful to prompt participants to take turns adopting the persona, relieving pressure off a single person and gaining an understanding of how others perceive the persona and their needs.

stakeholder hats

Playful   **Customisable**

When evaluating and refining your ideas, it can be valuable to consider how different stakeholder groups would respond to each solution. Create a series of hats representing key stakeholders – funding bodies, legislators or higher-ups who will be involved in implementing your solution. Distribute the hats among your participants and ask them to assume the persona of these characters, voicing any concerns or potential barriers. This process will strengthen your final solution.

TIP: *Stakeholder specifics*

If your participants are unfamiliar with the roles and priorities of your chosen stakeholders, you may want to give them some pointers before they assume the role. You could provide them with information about funding, existing legislation or current barriers to implementation.

the art of co-design

trigger
films

SIMILAR TO:
trigger videos

what

Editing video footage of interviews into a short, emotive film, used as a tool to motivate change and prompt discussion

why

exploring

Filming interviews that will be edited into a trigger film

ideating

prototyping

testing

sensemaking

provoking

Presenting the trigger film to other stakeholder groups to motivate change and prompt discussion

DIY

There are endless creative ways to adapt **trigger films** to suit your projects and people. Here are some of our favourites for inspiration.

film from interview

Accessible **Customisable**

Interview a number of participants about their experiences, filming the interviews with permission from those involved. You could film high quality interviews with a professional video camera, or simply hit record on Zoom and embrace the lo-fi look. Edit the interviews into a compilation film, either following the structure of the questions asked or weaving a more organic narrative based on the responses that emerge. Show the film to other stakeholders as a tool to generate discussion and encourage empathy.

TIP: *Work smarter, not harder*

You don't need a professional videographer to make a dynamite trigger film: programs like Descript allow you to transcribe a video then chop and change text to produce an edited film. This is often more than enough to convey participant perspectives in a way that feels authentic and genuine.

film in situ

Child-friendly   **Customisable**

If you have access to a videographer or a professional video camera, filming experiences as they are happening can make for a very powerful trigger film. Often this footage will be interspersed with "talking heads"-style interviews to paint a detailed picture of the participant perspective. This approach is best when the film will be seen by large, professional audiences.

TIP: *Avoid glossy tropes*

While bigger budget films sound good on paper, when conveying participant stories it is important that they don't feel contrived, over-produced or overly sentimental. Trigger films should be somewhat subversive and unexpected, bringing light to aspects of participants' lived experience that are not often shown.

citizen videographers

Scalable   **Low fidelity**

If a videographer isn't in the budget and you have access to willing participants, creating first-person films in which people with lived experience stand behind the camera can be incredibly powerful. You could use an approach like *mobile diaries*, asking participants to capture video footage as they go about their daily lives, or assist them in filming a specific experience. Involving participants in the filming and editing process means that they are completely in control of the narrative, crafting authentic stories.

TIP: *Provide pointers*

It can be useful to provide simple pointers to your citizen videographers. Remind them to film in landscape, provide them with potential topics or scenes they might want to capture, and give them the tools they need to craft an engaging story.

user
testing

SIMILAR TO:

usability testing

what

Providing participants with a working prototype of a solution to test its use and give feedback

why

exploring	ideating	prototyping

testing	sensemaking	provoking
Presenting a prototype to participants to test and iterate on		

DIY

There are endless creative ways to adapt *user testing* to suit your projects and people. Here are some of our favourites for inspiration.

think aloud testing

Speedy   **Customisable**

Ask individual participants to test a product or service, speaking their thoughts aloud as they navigate its functions. This would normally be done in a controlled setting, with a facilitator observing the testing session. This allows reactions to the solution to be gauged immediately. The facilitator can ask for clarification if they don't understand a participant's experience, or ask them to elaborate.

TIP: *Avoid distractions*

To avoid the participant being distracted or feeling self-conscious, try to sit outside of their immediate eyeline, preferably to the side.

a/b testing

Scalable **Customisable**

Create **prototypes** of two different solutions – these could be slight variations on the same solution or entirely different solutions to the same problem. Test one solution with 50% of participants, and the other solution with 50% of participants. You might conduct A/B testing informally, presenting different **prototypes** to different workshop groups, or formally as solutions that are trialled in practice for a set period of time.

TIP: *Control for other variables*

For A/B testing to result in the most meaningful insights, it's important to try and control other variables and use the same evaluation tools to assess solutions. In a workshop setting, this means presenting the two concepts in the same way, as well as involving similar participant groups and demographics.

asynchronous testing

Scalable **Accessible**

In instances where you are unable to access participants for in-person feedback, or you want a large number of people to test your solution, asynchronous methods may be appropriate. For digital solutions like apps, websites or interactive PDFs, you could provide participants with a link to a **prototype** alongside a feedback **survey**. For solutions designed to be used in their own environment, consider sending something resembling a **cultural probe**: a package including your prototype alongside prompts for participants to

TIP: *Use tech to your advantage*

There are many user testing tools on the market to provide more detailed data around participant engagement. For example, some apps track eye movements, creating a "heat map" to show which parts of an interface are most engaging. Alternatively, ask participants to simply record their responses with audio or video.

human-centred

AUTHENTICITY

playfulness

COMPASSION

HONESTY

empathy

curiosity

NO-NONSENSE

value mapping

SIMILAR TO:
value sorting

what

Mapping the personal values, perspectives and biases of the people involved in the project

why

exploring

Mapping the values of participants to understand how their biases will influence the project, documenting values that need to be represented in the project outcomes

ideating

prototyping

testing

sensemaking

Evaluating solutions against the key values identified in the "*exploring*" stage

provoking

human-centred   AUTHENTICITY

playfulness   COMPASSION

HONESTY   empathy

curiosity   NO-NONSENSE

DIY

There are endless creative ways to adapt **value mapping** to suit your projects and people. Here are some of our favourites for inspiration.

value card sorting

Speedy   **Customisable**

Create a diverse list of values and write them onto individual cards. Ask participants to sort the cards, ordering them from most important to least important.

TIP: *Use existing value lists*

There's no need to create your values from scratch: you can find many pre-existing values lists online. You may want to customise the values to your specific context, removing any that aren't relevant. Stick to around 20-50 values, depending on your context – any more could be overwhelming.

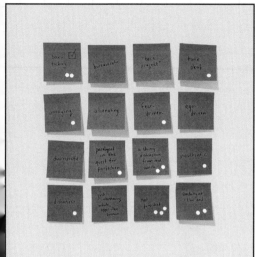

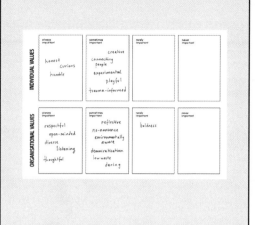

BYO values

Speedy **Customisable**

Ask participants to individually write values that are important to them on cards or sticky notes. Collect the cards/sticky notes, then display these and ask participants to select the values that are most important to them using a method like **dot voting**.

map your values

Speedy **Customisable**

Create a structured value mapping template to encourage participants to map their values across different contexts. For example, you might include sections for individual values and organisational values, ranked in order of importance. This could include personal values of participants, as well as perceived values of an organisation.

TIP: *Be specific*

Be specific with your prompts and instructions for this activitiy. For example, you might start with a question like "what values do you want your workplace to uphold?" or "what values do we want to communicate to our patients?"

TIP: *Custom vs template*

There are several existing value mapping templates you can follow. However, you may want to add your own specifics to the exercise so that it feels personal and meaningful to participants.

voting

SIMILAR TO:

multi-voting
sticker voting
dot-mocracy

what

Presenting participants with a number of prompts or ideas and asking them to vote on their favourite option(s)

why

exploring

Prompting participants to vote on particular aspects of an existing product or service, indicating where problems and opportunities lie

ideating

prototyping

testing

Using a voting system as a means of evaluating potential ideas and solutions while testing them

sensemaking

Involving stakeholders in the sensemaking process by asking them to vote on which insights resonate or matter most to them

provoking

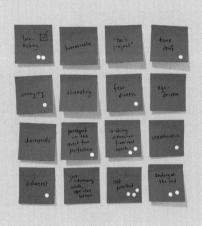

DIY

There are endless creative ways to adapt *voting* to suit your projects and people. Here are some of our favourites for inspiration.

the art of co-design

dot voting

Accessible   **Speedy**

Write a number of different ideas/solutions on separate post-it notes or pieces of paper, asking participants to place stickers on the ones they prefer. You could give participants one or multiple stickers, depending on the number of solutions. This is a fantastic way to get a birds-eye view of which ideas are most popular.

TIP: *Coloured dots*

To add an extra layer of detail to the activity, consider using different coloured or shaped stickers which represent different criteria. For example, you could ask participants to place red stickers on the most edgy or subversive ideas, while green stickers could be place on the most usable solutions.

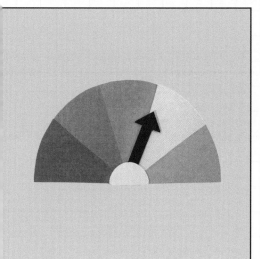

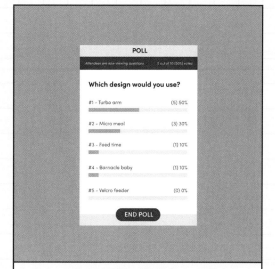

playful voting

Playful   Child-friendly

Create a playful and tangible voting device. This could be numbered voting paddles, a physical score or gauge, or a giant novelty thumb to turn up or down. Provide each participant with a voting tool and present them with a series of ideas, prompting them to cast their votes. This is a brilliant way to make the process of evaluating ideas more fun and engaging.

TIP: *Pitch to a panel*

When using a playful method in a codesign workshop, it's important to consider how the layout of the space might add or detract from the playfulness of the activity. Consider arranging seats to create a judge's panel, where participants sit to cast their votes. Consider whose role it is to stand in front of the panel and present each idea.

virtual voting

Scalable   Speedy

There are a number of ways to capture participant votes in a digital environment. You could create a poll using a website like Mentimeter, use the voting functions that come with virtual meeting tools like Zoom, create an online padlet, make a Miro board with a voting component, use social media to track likes... the list goes on! Some tools like Mentimeter can also work well in face-to-face workshops when you need to quickly poll the opinions of a large group, but be wary of introducing smartphones to a workshop environment!

TIP: *Consider qualitative feedback*

Consider if you need to create space for qualitative feedback alongside votes. For example, ask for a quick written response that explains a decision. This feedback could be given verbally if the voting is happening as part of a workshop, or you may need to choose a digital tool that allows for text-based responses.

world café

SIMILAR TO:

**knowledge café
group discussions**

what

Creating a "café" environment in a room full of small group tables, posing each table a series of questions, then asking them to share their insights with the room

why

exploring

Capturing insights by presenting a series of prompts to participants at tables among a larger group

ideating

Prompting rapid ideation by encouraging small groups to brainstorm before presenting their ideas to a larger group

prototyping

testing

Providing each table with a prototype for the group to review and evaluate together, summarising and sharing their thoughts

sensemaking

provoking

DIY

There are endless creative ways to adapt *world café* to suit your projects and people. Here are some of our favourites for inspiration.

world dinner

Accessible   **Scalable**

Normally the "café" in "world café" refers to the arrangement of tables in a room rather than the presence of food. However, if it's appropriate for your project and people, consider inviting consumers and stakeholders to a literal dinner, arranging them at small tables that allow for conversation. Throughout the dinner, pose each table a series of questions, before asking them to share insights with the room. This format tends to work well with a larger group of participants, generally more than 20.

TIP: *Thoughtful seating arrangement*

It's important to consider who should be seated at each table. You may want to cluster cohorts – for example having a table of doctors, a table of consumers and a table of nurses, so they can each come to a consensus. Alternatively, it is common to arrange mixed tables where many different voices are represented.

virtual café

Accessible **Scalable**

In lieu of physical "café" tables, virtual workshops can still be designed to encourage small group discussions. Invite a large group of mixed stakeholders to a virtual session, using a video conferencing platform. Introduce the entire group to the project and problem space before splitting them into breakout rooms, each with an assigned facilitator. Ask the facilitators to take them through a series of questions and activities. Finally, return all participants to the main room, asking a representative from each to present their ideas.

TIP: *Virtual scribe*

During large virtual sessions where many ideas are being shared, having a scribe who is taking live notes on a virtual whiteboard like Miro or Mural is crucial to ensuring that all ideas are documented, and that all participants feel that their voices have been heard.

feast or famine

Playful **Subversive**

To generate a bigger range of insights within a world café, tables may be divided so they examine and respond to problems and topics from distinctly different perspectives. For example, you can run the world café with a theme of utopia (feast) and dystopia (famine). Each topic is then viewed from both a positive and negative lens. This approach will allow negative perspectives to be captured in a lighter and more balanced way, without dominating a session.

TIP: *Ordering insights*

While it works well to assign opposing perspectives to different groups and collate what emerges, consider the order in which the groups share insights. It's generally better to lead with negative reviews and reflections and then close with a more positive viewpoint, to ensure optimism for the overall project remains.

getting
ready to
co-design

Once you have selected the right methods for your project, there are some final steps to consider before you are ready to start co-designing. The following section takes you through the process of recruiting participants, and covers everything you need to know about ethics.

recruiting participants

Once you know who your participants are and how you want to engage with them, it's time to plan your recruitment strategy. There are many ways to recruit participants, and this is something you should decide on collaboratively. Work with your co-design team and stakeholders to consider the best ways of engaging with your stakeholder groups. Having a variety of recruitment methods can benefit your project by expanding its reach.

recruitment options

social media posts
If you have access to existing social media communities that relate to your stakeholder group(s), create posts using images, text or even video to invite and captivate potential participants.

email invites
Send email invites to a database of stakeholders or via e-newsletters. You may want to connect with partner organisations who can support the project by helping to identify potential participants.

posters
Create posters with project information and put them up in public spaces that are frequented by your stakeholder group(s).

tips for creating recruitment media

Pitch to the language of the participant group. Online language evaluation tools can assist with this. Include multiple languages if appropriate

Employ bright & engaging graphics and imagery. Consider working with a designer to create your recruitment material so it stands out and raises interest

Be transparent and informative about the project, so nothing is left uncertain or ambiguous

Outline the full level of commitment (including time) and the sort of activities that would occur in the co-design

Make sure it is clear that the contact person listed is happy to answer any further questions about the project before the potential participant commits

additional pre-co-design media

Consider what else you will need to communicate to participants prior to co-designing with them, setting the tone for the co-design process to follow. You may want to send them additional information, introduce them to the project team or communicate the values or intentions of the project using videos, images or text. Using a more engaging and upbeat form of media like a video can help to develop a positive relationship with participants beforehand, heightening their excitement. Introducing your co-design team as people, first and foremost, is an important step in dispelling any feelings of hierarchy prior to co-design.

You may also want to send some introductory activities to participants, supporting their involvement within workshops. By coming a little prepared to a session, these participants may feel calmer and more certain they can contribute. Make sure to be respectful of the time committment required outside of workshops.

the art of co-design

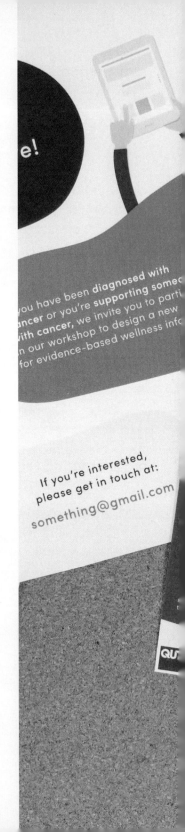

will you
need ethics?

Many co-design projects will require ethics approval before they can begin. Even if you decide that no formal ethics is required, it is extremely beneficial to reflect on a project from an ethical perspective. This provides a final opportunity to review your project design through a solely participant-based lens and foster a safe environment.

the art of co-design

ethical co-design

If you want to openly publish the findings from your co-design process and add to the body of literature in relevant fields, this will require ethics approval. If the co-design process is being used to inform a local quality and service improvement and does not meet the definition of "research", ethics might not be needed.

Depending on the project, formal ethics approval may occur through a health-based ethics body, a state-based education department, a university-based ethics committee or evaluation via an internal body within an organisation. The review processes may be slightly different for each. However, the requirements for each application are typically quite similar. If you are uncertain if ethics are required, or just wish to understand ethical guidelines, a strong starting point to access information is through the National Health and Medical Research Council (NHMRC), particularly their National Statement on Ethical Conduct in Human Research. While this is an Australian organisation, it offers a comprehensive overview of what ethical research is. Always spend time researching what type of ethical clearance may be required for your project and where to apply to receive it. Some of the principles that guide best practice in co-design from an ethical perspective are:

Ensure that all individuals involved are thoroughly informed about the purpose, methods and potential applications of the information and input they provide

Obtain formal consent from participants regarding their information and input

Uphold the principles of voluntary participation, where individuals are free from coercion and can withdraw at any time without need for justification

Safeguard the well-being of all participants, ensuring they are not knowingly subjected to harm or distress

Establish mechanisms to address any inquiries and complaints regarding the project and how it is being undertaken

Respect privacy and confidentiality as requested, adhering to appropriate measures to protect sensitive information

benefits, risks and mitigation strategies

A key aspect of ethics is examining a project fully and identifying its benefits, risks and mitigation strategies. It is important that a team does not minimise the potential risks of a project. An ethics application requires a project team to reflect on their methods and participants, and then consider realistic worst-case scenarios. This should relate to any risk, inconvenience or discomfort that the project might cause on a physical, psychological, financial or social level for participants, as well as the researchers and the wider community. Doing this makes a team consider the best ways to avoid or negate these risks in their project design. Mitigation strategies are then formally listed in their ethics application and are able to be applied if needed.

anatomy of an ethics application

In an ethics application, you will answer a series of direct questions about your project. You will also provide required documents, including those developed for recruitment or use by participants A standard ethics application will include:

protocol document

This document provides a detailed overview of the project, including the project background, key stages, participants and methods. It can be a critical document, as it captures the full scope and intricate detail of a project's design and its activities, which is not always captured in the rigid prompts of the ethics application. You can also include diagrams to convey the project design at-a-glance, alongside a more detailed written description of each phase. A final version of an integrated co-design map for a project may even be included here to provide clarity. The language here should be understandable to non-technical reviewers.

Phase 2: WORKSHOPS 1a, 1b

Co-design workshops with Health Researchers and Health Professionals (experienced in co-design)
Workshop 1a and Workshop 1b

Participants
Researchers in a field of child health and health professionals in a field of child health, working in community-based projects and health service design. All participants will have experience with or a working knowledge of co-design/participatory design/collaborative design methods. A preference will be applied for the selection of participants working directly within child nutrition research.

Participant Numbers:
Up to **5 participants per workshop**, with **2 identical workshops (1a + 1b)** being held to engage **up to 10 participants in total**.
NB. Smaller workshop groups have been selected to allow for a shorter time allocation for workshops (1.5 hours), which better accommodates those attending via Zoom.

Participant Recruitment:
Recruitment is via the professional network of the **Woolworths Centre for Childhood Nutrition Research**, using internal email lists for the distribution of a recruitment flyer to associated researchers and health professionals.
NB. As indicated, ideally participants in Workshop 1A will also attend Workshop 2A, and those attending 1B will also attend 2B. The recruitment flyer will invite participation in the 2 different workshops. Participants will be further informed about Workshop 2 and again invited to participate at the end of Workshop 1. No incentives are offered for participation in either workshop.

Mode
Blended Workshop – the workshop is designed to accommodate a combination of on-site (at QUT) and online (via Zoom) participants. Participants select a mode that best suits them. NB. QUT social distancing protocols will be followed when working with on-site participants
Adaptable model – Additionally, the workshop may operate with 100% on-site attendance or 100% online attendance, thereby responding to different group attendance preferences and any occurrence of a COVID-19 lockdown/an inability for the session to be held in-person.

Themes explored:
- Given what you know now about co-design, what would you like to have had to support your learning and capacity-building?
- Design a future experience for future researchers & health professionals learning co-design for an easier/ideal journey.

Facilitator:
Dr Jeremy Kerr (Chief Investigator)

consent forms

A consent form is a document signed by a participant to confirm that they agree to participate in activities, and that they are aware of any risks involved. The consent form will usually include an information sheet outlining the activities. When undertaking co-design with children, a team will normally ask for both the children and a parent/guardian to sign a consent form.

participant information sheets

A participant information sheet is used to explain the purpose of a project to participants, and what they will be required to do. They are usually distributed to potential participants with the consent forms, after they indicate that they are interested in participating. The ethics organisation reviewing your project will likely have a template that you can follow. These documents need to be written in plain language that is understandable to participants, and in some cases they may need to be translated into another language. If you are undertaking co-design with children and youth under the age of 16, you will normally need to provide separate information sheets for both them and their parents/guardians. You may want to include diagrams and images, particularly when explaining a project to young people.

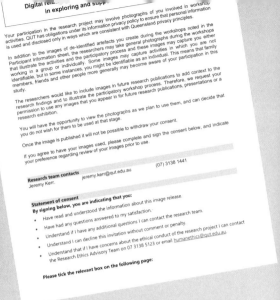

other forms

In addition to recruitment forms or details of recruitment media, you may need to include other forms for ethics approval. Templates are often available for these forms, which can be adapted to suit your project. These forms include:

image release sheet

This is a written agreement between a co-design team and a person depicted in any photography or video taken in a co-design process. By signing the release, that person gives permission for the team to publish the image or video in outlined contexts to display the project or process.

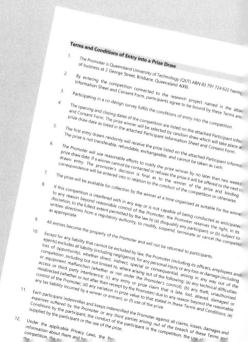

translator/transcriber confidentiality agreement

This is a legally binding document between a freelance translator and/or transcriber (i.e. someone outside the co-design team listed on ethics) that clearly states the terms of their involvement on a project. This document spells out the scope of work and the obligations of the signatory for their non-disclosure of any confidential information they have access to in the process of translating and/or transcribing.

---

prize draw terms & conditions

This is created in cases where individual incentives for participants to be involved in co-design might not be possible or seen as appropriate. To encourage participation, a prize draw can be offered for those returning signed consent forms and/or participating in co-design sessions. This form formally acknowledges the process for selecting winners of these prize draws.

---

withdraw consent form

This is a document to be completed when a person who is giving consent for the collection, exchange and/or storage of their personal information wishes to withhold some parts of their personal information and/or the personal information of any minors.

259

doing
co-design

Now that you have a detailed plan of what your co-design project will look like, it's time to do co-design! This section explains how to facilitate a co-design workshop, offering tips and tricks to help you set the scene for meaningful, creative and engaging collaboration.

being a facilitator

Regardless of whether co-design sessions are on-site, online or in a blended format, facilitation is key. In co-design, one team member is likely to operate as principal facilitator for a session. This person will guide participants through the planned series of activities, responding to the needs of participants as they emerge. Here are our top tips for being a dynamite co-design facilitator.

TIP 1   create a safe space

A safe space is a location (either online or on-site) which is free of criticism, conflict, and potentially threatening actions or conversations. Creating this space is essential in co-design as people are typically being asked to disclose lived experience, which might be deeply personal and make them feel vulnerable. The key to establishing this safe space is creating trust, developed through listening and displaying empathy. To create a safe space, consider:

Including an acknowledgement of lived experience at the beginning of a session

Operating as a mood checker, being alert to any topics and events that begin to distress or upset a participant, and changing the direction of the conversation if this occurs. Distress or upset may be apparent, not necessarily through what a participant says (or doesn't say) but through their tone of voice, body language or other actions

Offering post-workshop supports, such as a counsellor or service they can speak to if they need support to process what came up during the workshop. This should be mentioned to participants upfront in a workshop, so they are fully aware that this assistance is available if needed

Making it clear that participants are free to leave the space at any time with no consequence. It should also be made clear that they are not obligated to share personal experiences in the group environment

TIP 2   ensure transparency

To establish trust with your participants, it is crucial to be fully transparent about what a co-design session is for, what to expect in the session and how it sits within the entire project. These details should be reiterated at the start of a co-design session, even if they have already been outlined in participant information sheets. You should also explain how participants' personal data will be used, as well as the privacy and confidentiality protocols for the project. By detailing this, participants will be more relaxed and able to make an informed decision about their involvement in the project.

TIP 3   establish equality and abolish hierarchy

In co-design, everyone is considered equal. This means that power must be shared among participants within a co-design session. While a co-design team may not perceive it, a group of participants from a marginalised community may come to a workshop with a perception of hierarchy. Mixed stakeholder group sessions may present challenges in levelling hierarchies, and there can also be power imbalances and stakeholder tensions within organisations participants might come from. It is the facilitator's role to minimise hierarchies to ensure equal and open collaboration. Some established methods for sharing power include:

Introducing all participants and facilitators on the basis of their expertise and contribution, rather than position. This emphasises that being an "expert" comes in many different forms, from a "process" expert to a "lived experience" expert

Keeping it informal: dress casually, only include first names on name tags and keep a casual and friendly tone throughout the session

Being open and acknowledging power imbalances, stating that everyone has a voice and will be heard

Actively encouraging those who may remain quiet in sessions to have a say, ensuring all voices are heard

Keeping it simple: avoid complex use of language and complicated instructions and activities, including jargon and acronyms

Doing activities alongside participants, especially those which require a level of playfulness, silliness or vulnerability

TIP 4   manage conflict

Tension can occur not only within mixed stakeholder group sessions, but also ones involving a single stakeholder group. Participants in co-design are not the same, and will have different perspectives, views, and ideas – that is their greatest strength! To create a calm and collaborative environment, act immediately to deescalate conflict, while also acknowledging it. Conflicts can be crucial to understanding an area and the challenges within it. Encourage participants to handle conflict constructively, finding common ground and exploring new ways of thinking. Often a facilitator will act like a mediator, particularly when trying to find consensus around final decisions. You may struggle as a co-design facilitator if you are uncomfortable with conflict and actively avoid it; in this case we recommend undertaking a short study into conflict management prior to facilitating a co-design session.

TIP 5 prime participants for co-design

A facilitator needs to inspire a "co-design mindset" in participants at the beginning of a session. This means encouraging a sense of playfulness, creativity and risk-taking. By being upbeat and framing activities from a perspective of fun and exploration, you will motivate and excite participants to actively engage in the process. Encourage participants to be experimental, unafraid of sounding silly or far-fetched, and willing to try new things or think "outside the box". Within the session, promoting a positive attitude is essential to avoid ruminating on problems and their complexities instead of actively working towards solutions. You may want to play music while participants complete activities to bring the space to life, as well as completing activities alongside participants to show how they could be approached, rather than telling. Consider the specific needs of participants when setting the tone of your co-design space: for example, neurodivergent participants might find music distracting and struggle to concentrate on activities.

TIP 6 be flexible

A facilitator should be able to respond spontaneously to what emerges, exploring unexpected tangents and directions that deviate from the original plan. When interesting conversations emerge, be pro-active in asking further questions, following insights rather than manufacturing a discussion based on pre-defined topics. Flexible facilitation also involves "reading the room": sensing when a topic may be upsetting and may need to be reframed or moved away from. It may also mean adapting methods as a workshop progresses when certain planned approaches don't seem to work for the group. Planned activities shouldn't be delivered in a mechanical fashion, but should be adapted as needed, to suit the environment of the session. For example, if a group is not engaged in "making" activities, the time for these might be reduced, with more emphasis placed on follow-up discussions to generate insights and ideas. Don't be afraid to act spontaneously and intuitively.

TIP 7 manage time and follow schedules

While flexibility and spontaneity are essential to co-design, it is also important to keep an eye on the time so that key tasks are not missed. It is the facilitator's responsibility to adhere to workshop protocols, such as those outlined in ethics approvals, and to make sure workshop goals are reached. This will require setting estimated times for activities, and adjusting these estimates on the fly when changes occur. Being both structured and spontaneous is a challenging balancing act, and one that sometimes takes time to master.

When running a session, there is nothing wrong with reminding participants that there is limited time and moving on. You may use a timer while activities are being undertaken, in the spirit of a design "challenge" or "sprint". To avoid offending participants, or simply not having enough time to fully listen to a contribution, acknowledge that the group is moving on, but that the conversation can be picked up outside of the session. In managing a session, try to be conscious when discussions move "off-track" and steer it back to the agenda. If one participant is particularly dominating, avoid silencing them, instead redirecting the conversation and asking for input from other participants. This will avoid this participant feeling singled out or alienated.

facilitating with others

While a classic model for co-design workshops is to have a single facilitator from the core co-design team lead and run the session, there are other options that involve two or more facilitators, as well as working with others, which may be better suited to your project and people.

working with a support team

There are many responsibilities within a co-design session that a sole facilitator may not be able to handle on their own. By allocating these responsibilities to other team members, the facilitator can focus entirely on the task of leading a session without being distracted by practical set-up of the workshop. These tasks might include providing food and beverages, audio or video recording of the sessions, handing out materials, assisting participants during activities, welcoming people to the session, ensuring consent forms are filled in and managing tech difficulties.

One thing to consider is the ratio of co-design team staff to participants. While having additional team members on hand can help a session to run more smoothly, the number of participants should always be more than the number of team members present. Otherwise, participants can feel watched or studied. If a co-design participant group is particularly small, it's best to employ only one additional support team member who multitasks all roles outside of facilitation.

using an external facilitator

In some cases it might be more effective and appropriate not to have anyone who is part of the co-design team facilitate a session. Instead, you may want to employ an independent, external facilitator. You may seek out an external facilitator when members of the co-design team are not comfortable facilitating, are perceived to have a set agenda for a co-design outcome, or are concerned about their own bias.

lived experience facilitator

A representative from the stakeholder group might also be engaged as a sole facilitator, without co-facilitation from a member of the co-design team. Kitchen table discussions follow this format, establishing strong community relationships by facilitating co-design by, with, and within the community. This is a great way to build trust and create a space where authentic responses can emerge. You may need to provide additional training and support for a person with lived experience who hasn't facilitated a co-design session before, which will need to be factored into workshop preparation.

co-facilitating

There are many different reasons and ways to add additional facilitator(s) to a co-design session. Two main approaches are:

the art of co-design

alternative leading model

Having different members of a co-design team lead different activities throughout a session. This creates variety, and can be useful in longer co-design sessions to increase engagement, keep energy levels high and allow for facilitator breaks.

shared leading model

This involves two or more facilitators working with participants at the same time, much like co-hosts on a TV show. This can create an engaging dynamic, however it is important that both facilitators have a comfortable rapport and have planned how to approach activities together.

While co-facilitators may be members of the core co-design team, it can be more impactful to work with someone who has specific professional or lived experience. This may include:

counsellor, psychologist or other specialist

A support professional like a counsellor or psychologist can offer emotional support to participants during the workshop. This approach is recomended when members of a participant group might have experienced trauma or severe upset, or require specialised support. Including this relevant expert will help create a safer space and allow for immediate folllow-up if issues arise.

This co-facilitator may participate using either an alternate leading model or shared leading model. In the case of an alternate leading model, they may lead reflective activities to explore lived experience, using their expertise to handle traumatic or difficult material. The expert can explore these topics confidently and "read the room" to know when things should be moved on and conversation redirected. As well as supporting participants, this prevents the other facilitator from feeling out of their depth when engaging participants on sensitive issues. In the case of the shared leading model, the expert might be present throughout a session, but take more of a backseat role. They may participate if concerns arise, spontaneously guide discussion through emerging sensitive points and potentially divert discussion at appropriate times.

translator

A translator can support CALD or deaf participants during a session, affording them the option of being able to communicate in their preferred or first language. In most cases this co-facilitator will be employed in a shared leading model.

person with lived experience

This is often a preferred model for co-design, in which a representative of the participant group is actively co-facilitating. Co-facilitating with stakeholders can be especially advantageous in working with groups that are strongly community-driven. Some degree of training will be required for a lived experience co-facilitator if they have not facilitated a session before, and it it important to ensure you select someone who has both a strong rapport with any other facilitator(s) and a co-design mindset.

structuring co-design

While different workshops have different aims, timeframes, participants and modes of delivery, there is an intrinsic structure that underpins all successful co-design sessions. This section details the fundamental elements of a co-design session, applicable across all workshop formats, whether in-person, online or blended.

icebreaker	20 min
introductions	15 min
ground rules	5 min
activity 1	45 min
break	15 min
activity 2	60 min
wrap-up	10 min

STEP 1   icebreaker activities

An icebreaker is an exercise that aims to build rapport amongst participants, typically at the very beginning of a workshop. An icebreaker normally involves sharing personal experiences or insights, often in a playful way. The role of the icebreaker is to make people feel more at ease, connected and able to communicate, particularly if they feel nervous at the beginning of the workshop. Icebreakers do not necessarily link to the subject of the session, but can. Their focus is primary relationship-building.

An icebreaker should involve equal participation of all participants, usually through some verbal input, and they set the tone for everyone to be actively involved in a session. They immediately break the formality of the session and establish that the workshop is not like a standard meeting. Examples of icebreaker activities include a sharing circle (where a particular question is asked and each person answers while introducing themselves), introducing your partner (briefly learning about another in the group through a one-to-one conversation and then introducing them to everyone), or a creative activity, such as a collective drawing or collaborative building (creating models that attempt to solve a challenge using existing material). These latter examples are most likely to occur in an in-person workshop. However, online options for such activities include shared virtual whiteboards and other digital tools. Tactile activities can be successful within in-person workshops as they can bring an increased a sense of fun and create connection as people physically interact. Having a creative activity for an icebreaker can be beneficial as it serves as a direct lead-in to more challenging creative activities in the workshop.

There are many different types of icebreakers and selecting one for a workshop should be based on appropriateness and the abilities of stakeholders. We've included some examples of icebreakers to introduce participants to one another within our A-Z of methods. There is the opportunity for a co-design team to design their own icebreakers if they wish too.

STEP 2   welcomes, introductions, aims + agendas

It is important to set the scene at the beginning of a co-design workshop by welcoming participants and introducing the plan for the session. This could occur before or after an icebreaker, and is designed to provide transparency, orient participants and develop trust.

You may include: Acknowledgement of Country

Acknowledgement of lived experience

Introducing everyone in the room, or prompting them to introduce themselves, and acknowledging the unique perspective they bring

A brief outline of the agenda for the session

An overview of the project and what it aims to achieve

A brief explanation of the methods or approaches that will be used

Time for questions from participants

Including all these elements at the start of a session will make participants feel at ease as they no longer expect surprises in what is likely to feel like a foreign experience. Emphasise the value of participation to creating a strong starting point.

STEP 3   ground rules

Beyond basic welcomes, introductions, aims and agendas, you may also want to set ground rules for the session. Establishing these upfront can help to ensure a safe environment is maintained throughout a session. A facilitator might like to suggest some rules to start with, and then ask participants if they agree or would like to add anything to the rules, establishing a collaborative "code of conduct".

Rules could include: One voice at a time

Responding to a "quiet down" signal

No devices allowed

Discussions are confidential

Participants can leave at any time, without question

STEP 4   diverse activities

Typically, co-design sessions will include a series of linked activities, with one building into the next. It's important to have variety between activities, avoiding a sense of repetition and enhancing the mood of exploration and play. Alternate between group and individual activities, as well as making, storytelling and sensemaking. Giving participants multiple options within an activity – drawing, writing or speaking – will allow them to express themselves in a way that feels intuitive.

Activities are typically followed by sharing and discussion of what emerges from them. People can share after they have generated ideas through an activity, and they are less likely to feel 'put on the spot' than they would be in interviews or focus groups. Co-design data is then captured in multiple ways, through making, drawing and/or writing, as well as discussions.

Having different allotted times for activities, from fast activities to longer and more in-depth ones, can also lead to more dynamic sessions.

STEP 5   breaks

Generally, co-design workshops are at least an hour and a half long. For shorter workshops, a formal break might not be needed, but you may still want to have light refreshments on-hand. For longer workshops, especially those 3 hours or longer, a substantial break should be factored in to allow participants to recharge. Breaks are important whether participants are on-site or online, and specific break times and durations should be informed by the needs and contexts of participants. For example, children may need more breaks and periods of unstructured play in between activities. Providing appropriate catering can be an effective way to signal to participants to take a break and recharge and give purpose to the break. Where participants are having to sit at a desk for prolonged periods, you might also consider short 5 minute breaks involving physical movement every 45 minutes or so to avoid dips in energy and attention.

STEP 6   wrap-ups and thank-yous

It's always important to correctly wrap-up a co-design session, even when it may be rushed towards the end. Make sure you take the time to formally summarise key insights of a session to participants, as both a recognition of what was achieved and for validation and further feedback. Attendees should be personally thanked and informed of "next steps" and how they will be made aware of project progress and outcomes.

It is important to also remind participants that there are opportunities to debrief afterwards if needed. This could be offered in multiple ways: immediately after the session (where an appropriate person is available to them), or any time afterwards (via a phone contact or email). Having a clear process for anyone experiencing distress following a co-design session is a moral obligation, especially in projects where participants may have experienced trauma and distress in the past.

creating
collaborative
spaces

Beyond a workshop's structure and content, it
is also important to consider the delivery mode
– whether on-site, online or blended – and its
unique requirements. This section includes things
you will need to consider for each mode, in order
to create vibrant collaborative environments.

blended
co-design

creating connections

There is a distinct tension that can occur in a blended co-design session, where online participants may feel disconnected or deprioritised if vibrant discussions are happening on-site. On-site co-design facilitates greater connection with participants, and a facilitator needs to be aware of this tension to ensure they engage and include online participants equally. This might entail starting discussions with online participants and specifically asking them for input and feedback. On-site participants can serve a supportive role for the online participants by demonstrating how activities can be undertaken while the facilitator is explaining the activity. This allows online participants to become more aware and connected to on-site participants.

When it comes to planning breaks for the co-design session, online participants should be prioritised, as they will require more breaks than would occur for participants in a traditional on-site workshop. Aligning the breaks for both groups will reinforce that participants are one collaborative group, regardless of location.

managing tech troubles

The disconnect of online participants in blended workshops can be made even more pronounced if tech issues arise. For example, if on-site conversations are not easily followed by online participants due to sound issues or a poorly placed webcam, it can detract from their experience. Ideally, microphones should be tested to ensure all on-site participants are heard, and seating planned so that all on-site participants are visible to online participants.

Despite testing equipment, there is always a chance that issues may occur, or a participant may have a particularly problematic connection and not be able to participate as required. A back-up strategy should be considered for online participants, which might involve emailing pre-prepared instructions for the participant to follow during the workshop time.

on-site
co-design

spaces

It's important to select the "right" physical environment for co-design – one that is welcoming, collaborative, inspiring, functional, safe and accessible. Some things to consider include:

Choose a safe space that participants can feel relaxed in, and that they are not intimidated or triggered by. For example, a formal classroom at a university may intimidate some groups, while a meeting space located in a hospital may be triggering for certain participants due to their lived experience.

When mixed stakeholder groups are attending a session, it is important the space is neutral, not reinforcing power dynamics between the two. For instance, when co-designing with both service providers and service users, co-design should not occur at the service site.

To reduce anxiety levels for participants who might be particularly susceptible (for example, some people with autism or a background of trauma), co-design should occur in familiar environments. If this is not possible, a video tour of the space – with introductions from the facilitator – could be sent to participants prior.

Consider the physical characteristics of the space: it should be largely protected from external noise, have adequate table space and seating, and potentially allow "pin up" spaces on walls for activities or additional space for breakout groups.

It is important to prioritise accessible spaces, accomodating participants with disabilities whether they are disclosed beforehand or not. All venues should be wheelchair accessible, reachable by public transport, have wheelchair accessible toilets and have secure parking. Gender-neutral toilets are also preferrable.

Provide support for transport and parking needs to attend the workshop, either through travel tickets, parking vouchers or other equivalent incentives.

You may need to cover other additional expenses, for example longer-distance travel, accomodation and food if a participant is not local.

equipment

The equipment required for the space will be dictated by the methods and activities planned. It is important to consider and plan for both technology-based equipment and tangible workshop materials beforehand. Common equipment might include:

Electronic equipment	Tangible workshop materials
laptop	paper
projector	pens, pencils and markers
screen	sticky notes
microphones	white board
video or audio recording equipment for data collection	blu tack
	butchers paper
appropriate electric outlets for all computers and other equipment	templates and materials for activities

catering

In planning an on-site co-design session, one key budgetary expense is catering costs. Most people will require food and refreshments to maintain their energy and engagement throughout an extended session, and mealtimes can act as a valuable moment to socialise and connect with the group. A meal is likely to fortify a sense that everyone is part of a team.

Catering should be provided for sessions over 2 hours, particularly if a workshop occurs across standard mealtimes. For full day sessions (of about 8 hours), a standard of 3 catered breaks should be included. Catering should be healthy and meet the needs of all participants, accommodating special dietary needs and allergies, as well as religious requirements identfied beforehand. For shorter co-design sessions, drinking water and tea/coffee-making facilities should be provided for participants, with snacks as an optional extra.

online co-design

equipment + technology

basic equipment

In order for participants to participate fully in the experience of a virtual co-design workshop, it is important that they have access to appropriate equipment. Basic equipment includes computers with working cameras and audio, access to high-speed internet and necessary online video streaming software.

tech support

All facilitation equipment and technology should be fully tested beforehand with team members, and a delegated person should also be present at the session to identify and address any tech issues. As with blended co-design workshops, despite testing equipment, there is still the chance that issues may occur for participants during a session and prevent them participating fully. Devise a back-up strategy for these participants, which may involve emailing pre-prepared instructions for activities to the participant, so they can still complete these exercises while the workshop occurs.

virtual tools

There are a myriad of virtual platforms that you can use during a co-design session. Tools like Zoom and Microsoft Teams can be used to facilitate the session, while tools like Miro or Mural can be used to present activities and document insights as they emerge. Software in this space continues to develop and improve at a fast rate, so technology options should be constantly explored. Importantly, video streaming software will allow for a straightforward recording process for a session.

tactile activities

If you are wanting participants to undertake tactile activities, you could send a "co-design kit" to them prior to a session, containing paper, pens and any specific templates and physical materials. The easiest way for participants to return tangible responses to a co-design team is to take photos using their phone and email them. It is important to provide clear instructions for this, particularly if participants have low digital literacy.

virtual facilitation

multi-modal facilitation

Facilitation in online sessions often involves verbal instruction alongside the use of a shared screen that might have slides that reiterate steps for activities. This multi-modal approach to guiding activities and providing instructions is particularly beneficial if there are sound/connection issues; the visual material will support participants by acting as a constant reminder as they undertake an activity. When providing instructions, facilitators should try to keep them short and reiterate what is to be done. They should also recap comments from participants throughout a workshop to ensure everyone is fully aware of what is being communicated, avoiding any ambiguity created by sound or connections issues.

breakout rooms

If using breakout rooms for smaller group activities, these should consist of relatively small groups – ideally 3-4 people – so everyone has an opportunity to contribute. Larger groups can be more difficult for participants to manage online without a facilitator present.

allocating time

As there are fewer opportunities for small talk and off-topic conversations within an online workshop, it is common for online sessions to be completed in less time than in an on-site session. As such, when scheduling activities it is encouraged to reduce time estimates for online sessions. Importantly, shortening online co-design workshops is likely to make them more feasible and attractive to potential participants.

breaks

As with on-site co-design, breaks and refreshments can be integral in maintaining energy levels and engagement throughout a session. Due to the nature of using screens – with the body moving far less and a person's entire focus being on a screen – breaks are even more important in online sessions. At the start of the workshop, it is important to let participants know they can leave a session at any point for a toilet break or refreshments, or just to move about if they need to.

adapting to diverse participants

A co-design facilitator must be aware of the specific needs of diverse participants. In the *designing for co-design* section, we discussed how co-design approaches can be adapted for specific stakeholder groups. This section details strategies for adapting to diverse participant needs "on the fly". Typically a co-design team wants to have a diverse cross-section of people within each stakeholder group, and as a result they should be ready to adjust and adapt approaches.

TIP 1 proactively supporting participants

When a team is aware that a group might include diverse participants with different needs, it is preferable to politely ask participants of these beforehand, so workshops can be planned and designed accordingly. Asking about participant needs shows consideration and avoids assumptions. However, it needs to be done sensitively. It may be beneficial to discuss framing with a representative of a stakeholder group when drafting initial communications and questions. Making simple adjustments in response to the needs of participants can drastically change their co-design experience, enabling them to participate fully. Examples of potential needs include: needing large print to view documents, accommodating for poor hearing, having access to a prayer space during a session, or attending workshops with a support person. Providing this support should be considered across all types of co-design, whether on-site, online or blended.

TIP 2 strength and play-based approaches

Strength-based and play-based approaches can be powerful when working with people from marginalised or disadvantaged groups. Facilitating a strength-based co-design session means instilling a sense of belonging, regardless of their abilities, orientation, gender, ethnicity and background. Every participant should feel like they matter, their ideas matter, and they can make a difference. A strength-based approach actively encourages people to be their authentic selves, without feeling self-conscious. A strength-based approach is especially important when vulnerable, marginalised and disadvantaged groups are in mixed stakeholder co-design sessions, where another stakeholder group may be seen to have greater power or hierarchical position. Emphasising equal partnership and value in differing viewpoints is essential throughout such a session. Other approaches recommended here include probing and clarifying more than usual. This encourages a person to actively contribute to the best of their ability.

Facilitating a play-based co-design workshop means ensuring that nothing feels like work, instead emphasising joy, friendliness, and social connection. Think about how you can add a playful energy to a space – perhaps playing music, using stimulating images and visuals, and creating space for informal chat. Play is a beautiful way of maintaining attention and inspiration during a co-design session, particularly for participants who are averse to more academic or serious settings or get bored easily.

TIP 3   customising communication

There are many reasons why participants may have specific communication preferences, and we always recommend a multimodal approach to workshop activities that prevents an over-reliance on written communication or verbal discussions. A focus on sketching, play-acting, model-making and other visual tools allows communication to occur more flexibly. This can be a beneficial approach for all participants in a session.

As noted, when working with CALD participants, or LEP (Limited English Proficient) participants, language can be a barrier to collaboration. If a co-design team is primarily English-speaking, and co-design participant(s) speak another first language, it is ideal to have a translator present for the session or operating as a co-facilitator. It is also preferable that they come from the same cultural group as participants, as they are more likely to be culturally aware.

If they are not available, tools that can assist with communication include:

Google translate can be used to support any tricky aspects of communication, allowing language barriers to be overcome in a playful way.

Communication cards might be purchased or created to allow participants to identify any communication issues as they happen. For instance, these cards can have helpful phrases for cross-linguistic conversations, such as "I do not understand" and "Please talk slower".

Emotion vocabulary sheets may be helpful for specific co-design workshops, including a list of emotions – potentially in more than one language – with emojis. This will allow participants to quickly communicate their emotional responses.

Along with these approaches benefitting CALD or LEP participants, these can serve as effective strategies for co-designing with other groups that may find language-based communication and comprehension challenging, such as people with dementia or a cognitive difficulty, or young children.

ple of words that a person could have

rs later.

from the eating disorder project too,
So this expectation in the sense of
get solved. And if you don't have I
athy, if there's not that human
ere's not a real connection where
like you really working to a solution
g for someone because it's so
ou're talking about too, I mean,
t just about. It's not only child
zen we're calling them rather
tural change and stuff like
too, even while you wor
we going to initiate it

fficult to overcome. So I
aires? team. The
ns of I see my d
oring a range o
d so believe I was
roving how we care.
o make change. It's
either leading or
you do project
h a colleague or

aring a project
I think that
change

yeah,

sort of
thing that's sort of
nportant job, but
eople. So that
m, has dimini
ustralia has re
hink that workforce
d the workforce and
tralised health
think and maybe to
edibly
ospital if yo
ed convenie
s just easier to
much more
ne of your
we've got an

y pe

way of

It was also a
and actually
ening in differe

e kids
arn
el fairly
aven't
ink it's
ked

hich might not be s
o know I guess, you
like why would
ou're currently
ut any other
ub.

in the
actually
hich is a
m, but
er co-
o-
is is

to do, how does it look like

are ver~

aff will be

as

it

analysing + sensemaking

Once you have been through the co-design process and come out the other end, it's time to make sense of the rich data that's emerged. This section outlines some of the preferred methods for analysing and sensemaking co-design results, to help you translate creative collaboration into actionable insights.

how to make sense of data

While it may be simple to collate the results of some co-design activities, informing your next steps, others may be more complex and involve specific methods for analysis and sensemaking. This section includes some of the most popular and credible methods used by co-design teams to understand their results.

In reviewing co-design data, it is highly recommended that this process includes people who were not part of the co-design process, along with a facilitator who is more familiar with the nuances of what has occurred in workshops. A co-analyst may be independent and come from a formal research background, be part of the co-design team, or be a stakeholder with lived experience, who is guided across the analysis process if they are not familiar with the methods. Typically, both analysts and facilitator/s should start by working independently and iteratively, before comparing findings and insights and refining results together. This multi-tiered process helps avoid bias occurring in the final analysis.

Data analysis, in all its approaches, should occur with the knowledge that co-design is a process that utilises a smaller sample size to develop substantial qualitative data with rich and creative depth. Data should not be considered from the sole perspective of its sample size and statistical power (as with some other research methods), but by what is revealed through the combination of artefacts, recordings and transcript-based data. When examining the data, the artefacts – such as design sketches, journey maps, models, audio recordings, video recordings or transcripts – should be reviewed in tandem. This ensures that the review captures the insights from both the designed material and what was said about it.

Irrespective of which analysis method is used, a team should aim to share any interpretation of data with prior co-design participants for validation and further feedback. To do this, a team might even use creative methods, rather than simply report a series of findings. FFor example, you might collate data analysis into a series of representative personas, scenarios and journey maps to deliver a more "review friendly" format for the participants.

thematic analysis

WHAT Thematic analysis is a well-known method of data analysis. Thematic analysts examine all types of data collected holistically (visual artefacts, mock-ups, audio recordings, video footage of workshops, transcripts from workshops etc.). The ultimate goal is to identify *themes* (the key ideas and insights that can be found in the data, such as titles given to a collection of codes) as well as supporting *codes* (a word or a short phrase that represents an idea). A code encompasses a range of non-quantifiable elements, such as events, behaviours, activities, meanings, principles, features, etc. In the analysis process, codes are allocated meaningful thematic titles and may occur across all data.

HOW Thematic analysis is undertaken through a process of identifying, describing and reporting patterns, then delivering insights in an organised and detailed way as themes.

The process of thematic analysis commonly consists of the following steps:

1. Familiarising yourself with your data

2. Generating and applying initial codes

3. Searching for patterns and themes

4. Reviewing themes

5. Finalising and naming themes

There are two approaches to coding, which can be used together or separately:

Inductive coding is where codes are derived entirely from the raw data – they emerge entirely from the data itself with no pre-conceived notion of what they should be.

Deductive coding is a top-down approach where a codebook with an initial set of codes is created and used for coding, based on prior understanding of what is being looked for.

In practice, projects often combine a deductive and inductive approach to coding to categorise all meaningful data. Analysts may deductively start with a set of codes (things they are expecting and actively looking for) and then inductively produce and iterate on new codes. This can be challenging when the collected data is not in one form (i.e., just transcripts) but involves multiple formats. You may choose to undertake a tactile process of coding artefacts (or the artefacts themselves) alongside printed transcripts, using coloured sticky notes and corresponding coloured pens to code your data. Alternatively, there are many software programs that allow you to code multiple data sources and organise complex materials, including NVivo, Atlas, HyperRESEARCH, Max QDA and Observer.

the art of co-design

affinity mapping

WHAT   Affinity mapping is a method that gathers large amounts of written data (for example ideas, experiences, problems, etc.) and organises it into groups based on natural relationships. While it can be used within co-design workshops to generate data, it can also be applied by analysts to examine and understand collected data. As a process, it's extremely useful to dissect co-design data, especially in identifying design principals and features for emerging ideas. These can then be directly appplied to develop design solutions.

HOW   Place individual pieces of summarised data on post-it notes (either physical or virtual), then cluster similar or connected items based on their affinity to each other. Each cluster of data reflects a broader theme, which can be identified and labelled.

co-analysis

WHAT   Co-analysis is a process in which data is analysed collaboratively, with the project team and people with lived experience working in tandem. This approach can be applied to any of the previous analysis methods, and is increasingly considered the preferred model for co-design. Co-analysis ensures that stakeholder engagement occurs at all stages of the co-design process, allowing people with lived experience to validate and actively influence the analysis and sensemaking process as it happens. It is seen as a way to increase accuracy when examining data, ensuring that the bias and preferences of the team do not overly impact analysis outcomes. Another benefit of co-analysis is that it gives participants a greater sense of agency and ownership over the project – often these participants go on to be the biggest champions of co-designed solutions.

HOW   To conduct a co-analysis session, you simply need to bring a person with lived experience into the room, then follow any of the other analysis methods. It is important that co-analysis participants are properly remunerated for their time, reiterating that they will play an equal role to the project team throughout this process. Within some projects, people with lived experience may be employed solely to support the co-design team through the analysis process, offering their expertise to understand and interpret data alongside the team. In other cases, the team may select participants from the co-design process who are available and interested in being involved further. In some cases, a co-analysis process can also include representatives from multiple stakeholder groups (for example, both consumers *and* health professionals for a project in the health sector).

content analysis

WHAT   Content analysis is a broad analytical approach for examining qualitative and quantative data. While thematic analysis is a form of content analysis, it has a specific agenda: identifying reoccurring themes. Content analysis allows for greater flexibility in the types of ideas, insights and relationships that are explored. It is one of the most widely applied methodologies for interpreting meaning, and is used to identify key characteristics of data and present them in a clear way. It is particularly popular when analysing multiple media formats, such as text, photos, videos, social media and audio recordings. As with thematic analysis, there is the option to undertake it manually or digitally through the use of analysis software.

HOW   Content analysis can be undertaken in a number of ways, though all involve systematically categorising and coding content to identify patterns, themes, and relationships within the data. Types of content analysis include:

Qualitative content analysis: This method involves interpreting the content using subjective judgements and subjective categories. It aims to identify underlying meaning, themes and patterns in the data. It often involves coding the content based on concepts or themes that emerge from the analysis.

Directed/deductive content analysis: This type of analysis begins with pre-existing theories or concepts that guide the coding process. Analysts develop a set of predetermined categories or codes to examine the data. It is particularly useful when the objective is to test or validate existing theories or concepts.

Inductive content analysis: In contrast to directed content analysis, inductive content analysis does not start with pre-existing categories. Instead, it allows categories to emerge from the data itself. Analysts code the data without any preconceived notions or theoretical frameworks, allowing for new insights and themes to emerge.

Comparative content analysis: This approach involves comparing and contrasting different types of content or different sources of data. It aims to identify similarities and differences, patterns, and trends. Within co-design it might be used as a way to analyse and distinguish findings between different stakeholder groups.

Contextual content analysis: This type of analysis focuses on understanding the content within its broader context. It considers the social, cultural, and historical factors that may influence the production and interpretation of the content. It helps provide a deeper understanding of the meaning and implications of the analysed content.

sensemaking

WHAT   While analysis can often be quite scholarly and rigid in process, a more fluid option is sensemaking. This popular approach is typically applied in practice-based projects that do not have a research focus. There is no single agreed-upon definition of sensemaking, but there is consensus that it is a process of examining and understanding. Sensemaking loosely describes the process of understanding and interpreting data, then developing a series of practical insights from it. This process is more interpretive and impressionistic, identifying general themes rather than applying a rigorous formal analysis process.

While it is a quick and efficient process, and is typically used in projects not involving ethics clearance, there are safeguards to ensure the process is credible, and is not overly influenced by bias and subjectivity.

HOW   Sensemaking is generally made up of 5 stages:

1. Examining

2. Understanding

3. Constructing new knowledge

4. Making decisions

5. Leading to conclusions

Sensemaking might simply entail reviewing material and jotting down observations. However, it can also involve a process of clustering and categorising data, or a combination of both. Methods used in co-design workshops, such as personas and journey maps, can also be used as part of the sensemaking process: mapping data as a way of synthesising and interpreting. Another approach to sensemaking is to simply inspect collected data with the intention of creating a precise list of actionable items – for example, design features to include in a solution, or changes to be made to an existing prototype.

To ensure that sensemaking is credible, multiple people and viewpoints should be incorporated when examining the data, and findings should be presented back to co-design participants for critique or validation.

prototyping + testing

Once you have a good understanding of the problem(s) that need solving, and you have begun to imagine potential solutions, it's time to bring your ideas to life! This section explains how you can make ideas tangible, creating and testing them in practice as you iterate towards the final solution.

designing prototypes

A prototype is a mocked-up version of a solution, used to test whether it will work and to refine design ideas further. Prototypes are developed through an iterative design process undertaken by the core co-design team, potentially with external specialist designers and participants from workshops. Prototyping is a way to evolve something from what emerged in co-design with stakeholders, and an opportunity to expand and develop it into a more fully realised and practical form. Prototypes come in many shapes, forms and levels of fidelity, but there are three prototyping approaches that might be used throughout a project.

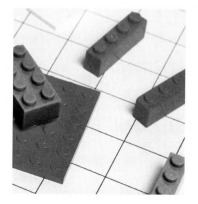

low fidelity prototype

Low fidelity prototypes are often created by participants in a workshop – think paper, pens, cardboard, sticky tape and pipe cleaners. Prototyping can also happen digitally – think virtual whiteboards like Miro or Mural, which allow you to quickly combine shapes, forms and text. The goal with low fidelity prototyping is to be "rough and rapid": communicating ideas visually as a way of bringing them to life to explore their features, strengths and limitations. A co-design team may follow up data analysis with their own development of low fidelity prototypes. You can prototype anything: a new product, process, intervention or service.

medium fidelity prototype

Medium fidelity prototypes are made once the project team have a good idea of the features and attributes that a solution should contain. You may take a low fidelity prototype from a workshop and refine it into a medium fidelity prototype, before presenting it back to participants for feedback. In most cases, this prototype will have limited functionality, but will showcase a variety of design features and the overarching conceptual approach. It should allow for testing and reflecting on multiple user scenarios. You could also create a proof-of-concept video, showcasing a design and guiding viewers through key aspects for feedback.

high fidelity prototype

After multiple rounds of iteration and refinement, the solution may resolve into a high fidelity prototype, which is presented back to stakeholders for feedback before creating the final solution. This is typically a computer-based prototype or a one-off physical artefact, taking you as close as possible to a true representation of the final design. You may create a mock-up interactive web site, refined communication media, a 3D render of a spatial design, service blueprints or physical pieces. A more detailed proof-of-concept video may also be developed here, operating as a realistic video tour of a design.

participant feedback

Once a prototype is developed, ideally the next step is to share it with some or all of the participants from prior co-design sessions. This check-in ensures that the prototype aligns with the shared vision and priorities of these co-designers, and that it's an authentic representation of their ideas. There are two ways to receive feedback on a design:

live feedback

Prototypes can be presented back to participants in an in-person, virtual or blended workshop, staging a design critique session in which they can offer feedback and revisions to the design. This is a great way of quickly ascertaining what works and what doesn't in a prototype, and agreeing on the next steps for the design. You may work with the same participants from a previous workshop, or combine different stakeholder groups in this session to encompass diverse perspectives.

asynchronous feedback

While some prototypes need to be tested first-hand in person, some can also be delivered and tested without direct contact with participants, which allows for more perspectives to be captured as it alleviates the burden of real-time commitments. With this approach, participants can review the prototype in their own time, in their own space, without the influence of other participants. For example, you might send an open-ended email survey with links to prototypes for review. You could follow this up with a one-on-one virtual interview or workshop if you want stakeholders to elaborate further, or simply implement changes based on survey data.

socialising prototypes

Following this feedback, and further iteration if needed, the prototype should then be distributed more broadly for review by other stakeholders. Ideally these are mixed stakeholders who have not been part of the design process, hence they have little to no prior investment in the design. The greater the number of stakeholder representatives that you "socialise" the prototype with the better, as they provide more opportunities to develop and refine the solution.

interactive showcases

You might choose to showcase the design to a large number of stakeholders, allowing opportunities for feedback. For example, this could be at an event, exhibition, part of a conference presentation or a virtual presentation with a live tour of the solution. You could host a luncheon or other social event, making the event more attractive, or simply advertise an informal gathering, which brings together mixed stakeholder groups to celebrate the partnership. Digital tools such as Mentimeter can be used to allow the audience to vote and provide feedback on specific features in real-time. Alternatively, you could take live questions and comments and provide opportunities for discussion.

focus groups

This is a more traditional approach for gathering feedback regarding a product, service, or concept, which has been used heavily across market research for decades. A focus group is a group interview involving people who have some common experiences/ traits. In market research, it tends to involve 6-10 people in a room providing feedback. A moderator will lead a 30-90-minute discussion within the group, designed to gather information. A focus group can also be held online, allowing for greater diversity in the group in terms of location.

digital platforms

Social media sites like Facebook have proven particularly powerful in gathering consumer feedback, as have other online tools like forums. This might be done publicly (supporting open participation), or occur in closed groups (via a closed social media group or site requiring sign-up or invitation). Online content will need to present a design in a clear and engaging way for review, and online polls can be used to gather quick quantitative insights.

co-developing + co-implementing

Now that you have agreed upon a final direction for your solution, it's time to polish it up and present it to the world! This section explains how stakeholders can be actively involved in developing and implementing ideas, contributing to the evolution from prototype to final product.

(still) working together

Having agreed upon a final solution, it's time to bring it to life through co-development and co-implementation. Continue to engage stakeholders during these phases, ensuring that the design evolves in a way that meets community needs and expectations, and that the expertise of stakeholders (including those with lived experience) continues to guide and inform critical design decisions. This means drawing upon your community of stakeholders to test, trial and give input as the prototype turns into a final product. Once released, stakeholders can also guide any further directions and iterations of the solution.

co-developing

It is common for a co-design team to engage stakeholders extensively in the ideation and prototyping process, however it is less common that they are actively involved in developing solutions. After initial ideas are produced and validated, often a co-design team may "take it from there", having gathered what they "needed" from stakeholders. Suddenly, the voice of lived experience is superseded by project leaders and staff. This approach is at odds with a co-design ethos, which centres on full stakeholder collaboration throughout the entire design cycle. Involving stakeholders in the product development phase not only embodies the spirit of co-design, but is often essential to the success of a solution.

Before embarking on the co-development process, it is important to identify what aspects of the final product will require feedback or contribution, by who, and when this stakeholder engagement should occur. You might choose to work with stakeholders to develop language and imagery, refine components of a product that have only been partially conceptualised and developed, or to ensure a product meets diverse needs. It is important at this stage to make a plan, which may mean revisiting and revising your original plan from the "designing for co-design" stage, and considering what co-development approaches would work best for your project now it has reached this point. Some collaboration approaches here include:

fit-for-purpose formats

Consider using more agile and customised formats than those utilised in the "front-end" workshops. Develop approaches that respond to what you have learned about your stakeholder groups. For example, you might seek individual asynchronous feedback. The flexibility of this often allows for greater stakeholder engagement, as they can determine how and when it occurs. Alternatively, you might try larger-scale, mixed stakeholder engagement, capturing a large amount of feedback quickly and efficiently, especially if this has proven successful in a previous phase.

Approaches might be similar to those listed in the "prototyping and testing" section: interactive websites, emailing "co-design kits", conference presentations, showcases, etc. It can be advantageous to respond to opportunities that already exist, using existing events that fit the context of the project as opportunities for feedback and collaboration.

consumer panels, steering committees or advisory groups

Establishing an "official" stakeholder group is a great way of formalising and recognising the contribution of participants, and it is a means for their ongoing input. There are many existing models for stakeholder groups, including consumer panels, steering committees and stakeholder advisory groups. These models acknowledge the role of stakeholders and allow for formal recognition so that involvement is more mutually beneficial. Participants can cite the role on their resume, using it as evidence of their advocacy and engagement in a cause that is important to them.

These groups do not necessarily follow a set format - they can be varied in how they function and how many people they include to best support a project. Some might involve asynchronous contribution, occur through attendance at meetings (online, in-person or blended), or involve more formal co-design sessions. They might involve a small, highly active group (potentially receiving remuneration at some level) or a large group representing diverse stakeholders. An advisory group, for example, might consist of hundreds of members. Such a large community of co-designers may be unwieldy for regular real-time meetings but allow for more flexible involvement for members, ensuring that no member is overly burdened. After the stakeholder group is established, you may want to form sub-groups of members who are assigned specific tasks.

Ideally, a team would invite prior co-design participants to be involved in such a group, as well as new representatives who could bring a fresh perspective to the work. Calls for participation from new members can be made in newsletter emails, relevant social media pages, invitations sent through organisational databases and networks, or "real-world" community posts and advertising.

mixed methods

While co-design approaches can be used exclusively, opting for a mixed methods approach is often more constructive. It is important to continue to use creative co-design methods when significant input is needed; however, you may also draw on more traditional consultation methods for specific project needs that don't require the same level of creativity. Methods such as interviews, surveys, focus groups and user testing allow for rapid feedback around particular features of the design solution, and can complement and supplement the co-development process. Such methods are all covered in our A-Z of methods.

co-implementing

After a final design has been released to the public, it might be reviewed, iterated and improved through further input from co-design participants. Actively involving stakeholders in the co-implementation phase helps to spot unforeseen issues and provide the opportunity to have these addressed and solved directly by those who will experience it.

Co-implementing can be approached in a similar way to co-developing. For instance, an advisory or consumer group may continue in its role on an ongoing basis, reviewing and developing a design as needed. Again, the formal recognition of co-design collaborators within this group can be an added incentive for stakeholder involvement through this phase. This also creates an opportunity for new users of the design to volunteer as members and help to improve the solution.

Active stakeholder involvement throughout this phase will improve the final product in authentic ways, plus it signifies the ongoing commitment of creators to their users and other connected groups, which will instil further support and goodwill.

evaluating + exploring possibilities

Your project is finally complete: congratulations! For some, this may be the end of your co-design path, but for many it is just the beginning. This section presents opportunities to reflect, de-brief and celebrate, as well as offering tangible next steps to continue your co-design crusade.

evaluating

Regardless of whether or not you will use co-design to develop future projects, it is important to thoroughly review your co-design journey to understand what worked and what didn't. This means reviewing and evaluating your project in full, using methods like exit surveys and debriefs. It is also important to celebrate the collaborative process as your project draws to a close, recognising all of the wonderful people who have contributed to the co-design process.

exit surveys and debriefs

Many teams integrate evaluation tools throughout the entire co-design process so that they can respond to participant feedback and adapt their methods if needed. Typically, this will involve short exit surveys at the completion of co-design sessions with participants. The focus of this evaluation is on the workshop experience itself, allowing participants to provide feedback on facilitation, the overall process, the activities and methods used, and whether or not the principles of co-design were respected and sustained throughout the experience. The co-design team will also debrief after a session, reflecting on what worked and what didn't.

An exit survey may also occur more holistically, at the end of an extended co-design process. Here participants will be asked to reflect on and evaluate the entire collaborative process they were involved in. While a simple survey may do the trick, there are also more creative options like mapping personal narratives or drawing impressions of the experience and its outcomes. While feedback tends to be individual, you could also facilitate a larger co-design focus group to reflect and explore how the project occurred. To show the impact of the co-design process, you may want to create a benchmarking survey for participants to complete at the outset of the project, then compare these results with exit surveys as the project comes to an end.

recognition and celebratory events

At the end of any co-design process, it is important to celebrate and recognise all who have contributed. A celebratory event is also a perfect way to share the final outcomes of the project, which is a requirement for most ethics-based projects. Celebratory events should be relatively informal, perhaps opening with a short talk to summarise the project and its outcomes and thanking everyone involved in its various stages, then allowing those people to mingle and socialise together. To ensure everyone is comfortable and can enjoy the event, members of the team might also act as facilitators for informal chats amongst guests. This will help to overcome perceived hierarchies and feelings of intimidation amongst those attending.

These events also offer the opportunity to capture the final impressions of participants on the co-design process and outcomes. A team might even consider holding open discussions, capturing the thoughts and opinions of participants on film. A video summarising the collaborative process can serve as further documentation of a project and recognition of its co-designers' contribution. Another way to recognise contribution is to apply for an award – many awards exist for collaboration in various sectors, designed to spotlight the contribution of people with lived experience to innovative projects.

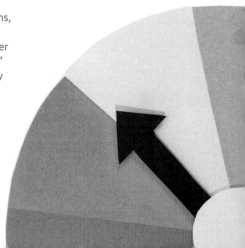

exploring future possibilities

As a successful co-design project comes to an end, it is important to consider if and how an organisation will continue to engage with stakeholders through co-design. There are two key ways to explore future possibilities: engaging stakeholders for ongoing reviews and defining future directions for the project.

ongoing reviews

After a successful co-design project is completed, there is an opportunity to build on this success and proactively plan to use co-design processes on an ongoing basis. For example, you could create a "consumer" council or committee, formally embedding co-design into everyday practice. The aim here is to continue co-design beyond an initial implementation stage. It may also be necessary to develop an improvement framework – potentially led by consumers/users and other stakeholders – to direct future engagement.

defining future directions

Co-design offers the possibility for stakeholders to define next steps for an organisation, including future priorities and areas of focus. In this way, co-design could be be used to define research questions or future projects to be developed and pitched for funding. Involving stakeholders in the conception of new projects takes co-design to its most collaborative potential – rather than deciding on new directions internally behind closed doors, stakeholders are involved as true partners. This signifies that an organisation is not simply collaborating, but is occupying a co-leadership role with people who have lived experience.

Congratulations, you've just journeyed through the entire co-design process!

bringing it
all together

There's so much ambiguity and confusion about what co-design is and isn't. Many people love the concept but don't understand how to apply it in a practical sense. Others are skeptical, and feel it's like opening a can of worms – bringing all of these other people and opinions into a creative and decision-making process. Writing this book, we wanted to be as transparent as possible about how we (and many others) approach co-design, showing the practical foundations while also celebrating opportunities for creativity and fun along the way. Even solving serious issues can be joyful when co-designing, tapping into people's creative spirit and collaborating in a playful way.

Co-design can definitely feel like an unfamiliar and murky process to undertake, especially for non-designers. The more that you practice collaborating in this way, the more it will become a natural way to work and develop better solutions. If you remain optimistic and continue to believe in the value of multiple perspectives, collective intelligence, and the expertise of experience, you are set for a successful career as a co-designer.

For those planning to undertake co-design projects in the future, we hope this book has provided a strong starting point. At the same time, we'd really encourage you to see creative possibilities beyond it. There exists no set formula for co-design, and no limitations in how it can grow as a field. Co-design is not black and white or one-size-fits-all, and it comes in many shapes and forms. We've tried to make that clear by showing you the options you have at each stage, and how the methods you use can be adapted, customised or reinvented to suit your unique project needs. Co-design projects, although being led essentially by stakeholders, offer tremendous scope for creative innovation from those initiating the collaborative process. As someone embarking on a co-design collaboration, you have the option of designing new processes and methods that best suit your participants, facilitating collective dreaming. While this may not be something you wish to explore radically at the beginning of your co-design journey, as you find your feet, we hope you'll join us in growing this exciting new field. We encourage you to build upon the foundation we've presented, put your own stamp on creative collaboration, and champion its use in all sorts of contexts.

If you see a problem that feels unanswerable – something that nobody has found a satisfying solution for – this could be the right place to start your co-design journey. When no other options seem to exist, why not try co-design? Why not empower the people most affected to band together and reimagine their reality? You will be delighted by what emerges.